A YARD LONG

A Natural and Cultural History of One Small Yard

Susan Rae Sampson

RIVERFEET

Riverfeet Press
Livingston, MT
Abingdon, VA
Bemidji, MN
www.riverfeetpress.com

A YARD LONG

A Natural and Cultural History of One Small Yard

Susan Rae Sampson

Non-Fiction: Natural World, Gardening, Birding, Ecology

Edited by Daniel J. Rice

ISBN-13: 979-8985398892

LCCN: 2024940185

This book is available at a special discount to booksellers, librarians, and educational institutions. Contact the publisher for orders: riverfeetpress@gmail.com

Typesetting by Daniel J. Rice
Cover design by Creative Pear Graphic Design, LLC
www.creativepeargd.com

CONTENTS

To my family and to my friends—you know who you are.

A YARD LONG

*A Natural and Cultural History
of One Small Yard*

Susan Rae Sampson

PREFACE

Looking for the Universe in a Grain of Sand

"To see a World in a Grain of Sand
And a Heaven in a Wild Flower,
Hold Infinity in the palm of your hand
And Eternity in an hour."
-William Blake

When the Covid-19 pandemic compelled us to stay home, I decided to use the time to take a close look at my yard. I was also taking a cue from Henry David Thoreau:

"I went to the woods because I wished to live deliberately, to front only the essential facts of life, and see if I could not learn what it had to teach, and not, when I came to die, discover that I had not lived."

I've read good examples of the kind of book I wanted to assemble. David George Haskell was inspired by Blake's poem and by Tibetan monks creating an elaborate, but ephemeral, sand mandala. He observed a one-meter circle in a forest and documented what he saw for one year. Jennifer Owen documented the flora and fauna of her English garden, a serious academic exercise, for fifteen years.

E.B. White put it succinctly in *Charlotte's Web:* "It is quite possible that an animal has spoken civilly to me and that I didn't catch the remark because I wasn't paying attention."

I planned to go slowly. I'd been advised before to slow down. When I took a photography class, I expected the teacher to encourage using a fast telephoto lens to capture distant fleeting images. Instead, he said that my first purchase should be a tripod to help me hold the camera very still. So, I resolved to stop and smell the roses, see the mammals, hear the birds, feel the sun's warmth and the wind's chill. I would remember the invertebrates.

REFERENCES

Blake, William, "Augeries of Innocence"

Haskell, David George, *The Forest Unseen, A Year's Watch in Nature*, New York, Penguin Books, 2012.

Owen, Jennifer, *The Ecology of a Garden, The First Fifteen Years*, Cambridge, UK, Cambridge University Press 1991.

Thoreau, Henry David: *Walden*, "Where I Lived and What I Lived For."

White, E. B. *Charlotte's Web*, Harper Brothers, 1952.

Part I

The Physical Environment

CHAPTER 1

Getting Updated

When I was last a biology student, all of life that I might expect to find in my yard, or even my entire environment, was divided into only two kingdoms: Plants and Animals. Fungi admittedly were odd but were assigned to the kingdom of plants. A fellow student gave me a mnemonic device for remembering the classification of living things within those kingdoms: Kings Play Chess On Fine Green Sand: Kingdom, Phylum, Class, Order, Family, Genus, Species. Or, as a professor said, "Kids Prefer Cheese Over Fried Green Spinach." But when I picked up a modern biology book, I was astonished to learn that although the smaller classifications remained the same, life is now classified into domains that are broader than kingdoms of plants and animals. The new domains were *Archaea, Eubacteria,* and *Eucarya.* Very roughly, they are single-celled organisms with no nuclei in their cells; single-celled organisms with no nuclei and rigid cell walls; and multi-celled organisms with cells having nuclei. Plants and animals are still kingdoms, and fungi are now a kingdom, but now there are more kingdoms, maybe as many as twenty. Studies, especially of DNA and stages of development, are ongoing. Everything descending from a node in the tree of life belongs to its "clade," a word for relatives up the family tree, a word that I'd never seen before, except in a New York Times crossword puzzle. Although classification tries to follow the physical features of organisms, life is so diverse, crossing so many lines of description, that classification is a convenience, but necessarily somewhat arbitrary, and constantly changing.

Not having a good microscope and attendant skills, I wouldn't be making a close examination of the archaea or bacteria from my yard, although a study of soils bacteria would be fascinating. The 20th Century was the age of discovery of antibiotics, like penicillin, streptomycin, and erythromycin, derived from molds found in soils, and more are out there yet to be discovered. However, the emphasis in medicine is shifting dramatically to gene editing and use of rDNA, so soils, molds and bacteria, and their medical applications, remain to be discovered.

On the other hand, I wouldn't want to get too close to some bacteria, anyway, like *E. coli* or *Salmonella* of food poisoning fame. I'd already met *Clostridium difficile* the hard way, and I'll scrub as if for surgery when I come inside after a day in my garden. I'll scrub thrice on manure-spreading day.

I won't see microbes, but my yard should show me plenty of *Eucaryotes*, including plants, animals, fungi and maybe a few more.

Flaunting my newly acquired understanding, I told somebody that kelp, a giant seaweed, was now neither plant nor animal. "Then what is it?" she asked.

A scientist might have answered, "An alga in the domain of *Eukaryota*." "A creature," I answered, because that term expresses more of the awe I feel when I realize that an organism I am examining is neither plant nor animal, but a life form that I've never thought of as being neither plant nor animal before.

REFERENCE

Tudge, Colin, *The Variety of Life,* Oxford University Press, New York (2000).

CHAPTER 2

How the Light Gets In

The vernal equinox fell on March 20 this year. We lie at 47.42 degrees north latitude, just two degrees northerly of the 45th parallel, which is the halfway mark between the Equator and the North Pole. That halfway mark is noted on a sign next to the I-5 Freeway near Salem, Oregon, about 138 miles south of us. However, we are still awakening in the dark; officially, sunrise comes at 7 a.m. and sundown falls at 7 p.m. Our actual sundown arrives a little earlier than the official time because the sun drops behind the Cascade Mountains and light fails us in the Wenatchee Valley. I grew up just one degree south of the 45th parallel, and here, just three degrees farther north, the changes of light that I see between solstices feel dramatic. The further north we go, the more extreme the changes in light become.

Once I had occasion to be in Anchorage, Alaska in the winter, on a work assignment. There, I had no sense of direction; I felt like the sun never rose. A few years later, I escorted my mother to Alaska in the spring to visit my sister's new son. Mom and I sat up late, visiting later than we would normally, while my sister, her husband, and the children wisely turned in. When 11 p.m. rolled around, we realized that we should try to get some sleep despite the pale gray sky telling us that it wasn't bedtime yet.

Somewhere a scientist has probably studied the human physiological response to our annual change of exposure to full spectrum light, although I expect that now, more studies are going into the exposure of light from computer screens. I appreciate my son's comment on hours of light: "My environment is always 72 degrees and fluorescent."

Our location in North Central Washington State is truly a four-season environment. It is too far inland for us to feel the influence of the Pacific Ocean that tempers maritime climates. There, seasons merge gently, one into the next. Here, the seasons turn so remarkably on cue that I once wrote a verse about the autumnal equinox:

> Today beside the Wenatchee River
>
> clouds descended below the tops of hills.
>
> Three days ago the sky was blue.
>
> Three days ago, the calendar said
>
> "Autumn begins."
>
> I wonder how the clouds knew?

March is still too early to do much gardening. The clerk at a plant nursery told me, "I'm from Montana. We have almost winter, winter, still winter, and highway construction season." March is still wintery here.

Traditionally, gardeners in the U.S. prune their roses on George Washington's birthday, February 22. I prefer to do my pruning when I see buds developing so that I know for sure which branches have survived the winter. In late March, the buds are just coming out. The tips of tulip leaves and the blades of irises are just appearing. The earliest peony has sent up stems topped with balls of leaves looking like clenched fists. The red knobs of the rhubarb are just beginning to push aside the duff that has fallen on them during the winter.

I can't turn the compost, though; it is still frozen, locked as hard as stone by the tremendous strength of ice. (We once filled the bed of a pickup truck with bags of trash under a canopy that leaked. When we got to the garbage transfer station, we couldn't move the bags. They were frozen to the truck. If there isn't a technology for applying ice instantly to glue things together, and for melting it instantly to detach again, then there should be.)

For now, gardening means just cleaning up the debris the winter wind has brought in. I recognize the leaf of an ornamental oak from two blocks away. There are no trees in my yard; there were none when I moved in, and I haven't grown any. I thought of planting a native wild cherry, but I didn't want to plant a tree that I might have to spray. Wild cherry hosts the same pathogens as domestic fruit trees and our state's laws require management with sprays as needed. I did not want to host a source of some kind of disease that might affect some of the many square miles of our neighboring orchards. I've seen a neighboring orchardist drive up with her handyman, cut down, and pull out a scrub apple tree from the undeveloped lot next to mine, which isn't her lot. She blamed it for the loss of that part of her apple crop closest to the scrub. She was taking her chances in cutting it down without permission. In this state, cutting another person's tree or shrubs exposes the perp to a lawsuit for triple damages.

The steady March winds have uprooted tumbleweeds out of the lot next door and tossed them like balloons over the fence, completely covering my compost cribs and the 10 foot space between my back fence and my garden shed. I have to crush them to stuff them into bags for garden trash rather than compost them. They say each plant can produce a quarter of a million seeds, and I don't want them to survive composting and take root all over my yard.

I learned after I began gardening here that some garden plants can be selected according to their preference for long hours of daylight, while others thrive with just twelve hours per day. Some seed catalogues specify which are long day plants. Particularly, there are potatoes and onions that thrive on our long summer days.

I've seen photos of cabbages coming out of Palmer in the Matanuska-Susitna Borough in Alaska whose hours of daylight during the summer put ours to shame. Their cabbages look big enough to hollow out and live in, like the wife of Peter Peter Pumpkin Eater, or to ride in, like Cinderella's coach.

Although seeds are usually sprinkled on the ground and tucked under a thin layer of soil to keep them from blowing away, some of them require light to germinate. As Leonard Cohen sang, "There are cracks in everything/ that's how the light gets in."

CHAPTER 3

Rocks of Ages

In the beginning of his novel *Hawaii,* James Michener described the origins of the Hawaiian Islands beginning with lava pushing up from the ocean floor, and birds dropping seeds on the emerging land mass. I can't start that far back like Michener did because the major geologic upheavals that shaped our topography today occurred a mere 10,000 years ago. *Home sapiens* lived here then, as they had since about 14,000 years ago, knapping their Clovis points.

Millions of years ago, three tectonic plates collided to create this part of North Central Washington State. They are the Pacific Plate, the North American Plate and the Juan de Fuca Plate. The latter was named after a Greek explorer sailing for Spain. When the plates crunched, they created the Cascade Mountain Range immediately to the west of us. Foothills lie between us and the Cascades. To the east lies a vast plateau comprised of layer after layer of basalt, once magma spewed by volcanoes and flowing over all of eastern Washington and much of Oregon.

The Columbia River formed a valley between the Cascade foothills on our side of the river, and the basaltic plateau on the other. From time to time, the Columbia River and its tributary the Snake River have been blocked by ice dams, creating massive water reservoirs. Possibly the largest was Ancient Lake Missoula. When the dams broke, they sent surges of water downstream in such volume and with such velocity that all of the extreme eastern part of Washington State was left a channeled scabland, an area bare of soil and gouged with ancient drainage channels. Scars on the rock wall at the Wallula Gap, near the confluence of the Snake and the Columbia Rivers, show that the floods could have occurred more than forty times. The numbers are imprecise because higher floods would erase the scars of older floods that weren't as deep.

Locally, the Columbia was dammed at Rock Island, about four miles downstream from my site. The lake behind the dam rose thousands of feet up the foothills. But then the ice dam lifted (ice floats) and the water impounded in Ancient Lake Wenatchee (not today's Lake Wenatchee) spewed out with tremendous velocity. Granite boulders resting on ice floats, called "erratics," were deposited on hillsides. When the drainage of the reservoir reduced water pressure on adjacent hillsides, the hillside at Malaga, WA, slumped. A landslide ten miles wide resulted. That's what shaped my mere 10,000 year-old yard.

For years, the Great Malaga Slide was one of the largest land movements known to man. By now, similar slides have been found around the world, thanks to satellite imagery; but the Malaga slide remains one of the largest. The land of the Malaga Slide, like old glacial till, is a mixture of rocks and sand and makes a decent base to build on.

No doubt the person who constructed my house used a grader to flatten the building site. It's a corner lot with a rounded corner and abrupt drop-offs on the north and west sides, with an undeveloped 50 foot wide lot on the south, and a low terrace and dense cedar hedge on the east. That's perfect—it shelters me from neighbors, but also leaves a wide bed of native soil in the backyard from which I can dig rocks.

We bought this house and yard in 2007 then moved in full time in 2009. When we moved in, the flower bed on the east was barren of flowers, or of any flora. It was covered with black plastic intended to block growth. I disposed of that.

When I began to dig in the formerly plastic-covered yard, my husband Jerry furnished me with an electric rototiller, small, suitable to my size and ability to handle machinery. Soon, however, we read that for gardeners, it would be a mistake to till the surface layer of a garden too deep, too often. Worms and other organisms that feed on organic garden waste would be lost. I shifted to a shovel.

I dug up rocks, endlessly, pebbles, fist-sized stones suitable for David's sling, and cobbles ranging from the size of a grapefruit to the size of a cantaloupe, almost as big as my head. As I excavated them, I tossed them into a wheelbarrow and used them to refresh the river rock landscaping that lined the entire foundation of the house. I calculated that I moved at least a half ton of rock.

Nearly all of the rocks I uncovered were rounded, chipped and sanded smooth from their rough ride downhill when all of Malaga slumped. Their mix of sizes revealed their sudden deposit, before the bigger ones had time to settle out.

The composition of those rocks was as diverse as could be. Those rocks had to reflect the content of rock uphill predating the Great Malaga Slide when those tectonic plates collided. They were already highly mixed from some prior cataclysm. They included granite, which is a black, gray, and white flecked igneous rock formed from volcanic output. They included limestone, a sedimentary rock, and its metaphoric form, marble. They included schist and gneiss, metamorphic rocks that started out sedimentary then were cooked into their existing layers. They included sandstone in the form of concretions, balls built up like snowballs, layer after layer, often alternating layers of dark reddish sand with layers that were gray. I found one rock that looked like the fossil of a mussel with its aerodynamic form and even some of the blue color of the mussel shell, and one rock that is clearly a lump of coral from a reef.

From the mix of rocks I find in the Malaga Slide, I can barely imagine the great mixing of rock that occurred uphill from here before the great slump. I have hiked in those hills, and I have seen small boulders of conglomerates, sedimentary sandstone studded with pebbles of metamorphic smooth-tumbled agate. I wondered what happened to mix such rocks even before the slide, and how many times they had been mixed before. I found the perfect leaf fossil from a piece of split sandstone, slipped it into my pocket, and took it home.

Poet Ray Sharp asked about me, "Why would she write about rocks? "

I do not understand his question. How could I not be interested?

REFERENCE

Mason, Charles L: *The Geological History of the Wenatchee Valley and Adjacent Vicinity,* 2d. Ed. Wenatchee, The World Publishing Co. (2006).

CHAPTER 4

Every Breath We Take

Astronomer Neil de Grasse Tyson tweeted, "Thin Air. The size of Earth's atmosphere relative to Earth is the same as the skin of an apple relative to the apple." Our thin skin of air is actually a mixture of moisture, dust, spores, pollen and pollutants. Still, our air looks clear for miles, unless it's one of our relatively rare days of precipitation in the desert, or unless it's a day with wildfires burning nearby.

In spring, a sweet aroma of Black Cottonwood wafts into the yard; their nearest stand is about three blocks away, but the scent carries. The cottonwoods also launch downy cotton-covered seeds, enough to drift past the window like feathers and to pile along the edge of the street like snow.

There is more in the air. Friends with allergies suffer when many square miles of nearby forest, orchards, prairies, and wheat fields bloom and their pollen goes airborne.

There is even more. A generous amount of loess, windborne particles of eroded minerals, blows into the yard to make our soil rich. Enough dust blows to partially cover the landscaping rock around the house. I have to dig it out, down to the underlying ground cloth every couple of years, or the accumulated soil will be deep enough to support a growth of weeds.

In *Gathering Moss,* Robin Wall Kimmerer says that spores from mosses float in an air mass that traverses the entire world.

In the spring of 2023, a mass of offshore air moved over the American Southwest, ending a drought, flooding southern California, and even depositing 4 inches of snow at Vail, Arizona, on the last day of February. Weather forecasters called it a "river of air." Rivers move matter. The term "river of air" does suggest that our clear-looking air is a veritable slurry surging over the yard-- injecting, infecting, and connecting us a great deal of the rest of the world.

REFERENCES

Kimmerer, Robin Wall: *Gathering Moss, A Natural and Cultural History of Mosses,* Corvallis, Oregon State University Press (2003).

Tyson, Neil De Grasse, tweet: April 22, 2016, 8:30 a.m.

Part II

Fungi, Lichens, and Moss

CHAPTER 5

The Fungus Among Us

Mildew and mushrooms are the common fungi that I find in my garden. If I expanded to talk about indoors, I'd have to add blue penicillin mold that grows on old bread, the black smut that develops on onion skins in the pantry, and maybe something lost in the back of the refrigerator, commonly called "a science project."

Outdoors, powdery mildew paints a white coat on the leaves, young stems, and buds of the Perfume Delight rose. I see where it's coming from. Across the yard, the prior owner of my house planted a grafted hybrid tea rose that died back to the rootstock. That rootstock has survived, and even thrived. It's a plant called "Dr. Huey," and sends up long, slim canes that bloom once in the spring. The flower is dark red, has five petals, and has no perfume. It is vigorous enough that it can climb up trees. I see it all over the neighborhood and all over town where owners might not realize that this is not the plant they selected from the nursery and intended to grow. It's pretty enough during its short blooming season, but it harbors mildew. It's the Typhoid Mary of roses; it infects its susceptible neighbors, including the "Perfume Delight" hybrid tea rose. I rip it out of my garden, but it's persistent enough to keep coming back.

The plant nursery offers fungicides for sale, but they come with warnings, and for my non-commercial hobby garden, that's just overkill. I once saw a friend praying a rose in his yard with a nontoxic mixture of milk thinned with water. He said it would protect against powdery mildew. I haven't had to try it yet.

The familiar symbol of the fungus is its fruiting body, the mushroom. It's just an apple on a tree, the tip of an iceberg, developing from a massive underground growth called "hyphae." Scientists have tried to trace the extent of hyphae and say that a hyphae mass in the Oregon forest may be the biggest single organism on the planet, bigger than a Blue Whale. (The competitor for largest organism is a grove of genetically identical aspen trees from a single base.)

In relatively recent years, scientists have determined that most plants, possibly all of them, grow in association with fungi penetrating their roots. Notably, our local tumbleweed has been described as having no known fungal symbiont. Fungi provide nutrients from soil to plants, which then produce sugars from photosynthesis to feed the fungi. Specific fungi species are matched to the specific plants species they support. Fungal reproduction is weird. Fungi exchange genetic matter with one another directly from one hypha to another, besides spreading by spores.

When the little dog-run area of lawn in my backyard gets

too wet, fragile little mushrooms pop up, shaped like half-opened umbrellas. The one other mushroom that sprouts up in my yard crowds the fence near the compost pile. It's a more substantial meadow mushroom, four inches across on a thick stem. Its gills on the underside of the cap are pink at first, then develop into a rich chocolate brown. My guidebooks say that it is edible, but I won't be trying it. First, it's critical to identify edible mushrooms with perfect accuracy because some are poisonous. Second, I don't know what traits a supposedly safe mushroom may have developed by exchanging genetic matter with other fungi in the neighborhood. (It's what the health department says about sex. When you sleep with one person, you are sleeping with everybody else he or she has slept with.) Third, I don't like mushrooms.

During the hippie era, my sister Sandy claimed that the threat of mushroom poisoning was exaggerated only because some mushrooms, like shaggy manes, were hallucinogenic. People feared hippies would consume them and go mad. The Uniform Controlled Substances Act tries to keep us away from that. It's true that some people invite those hallucinations. (LSD was developed to be medicinal and was found to be useful in treatment of anxiety, depression, and alcohol addiction. A friend was treated with an LSD derivative to prevent cluster migraines.) Farmers complain of trespassers raiding their fields at night, looking for hallucinogenic psilocybin mushrooms that grow in horse manure. In 2020, the State of Oregon legalized the use of psilocybin for treating PTSD.

I defer to the expertise of my brother, the emergency room physician, and refuse to test the psychological effects of eating mushrooms. He wrote his medical school research paper on the ER treatment of mushroom poisoning. He tells me that some mushrooms cause gastric upset. Some morels contain a substance that is chemically similar to rocket fuel that needs to be cooked out before the mushrooms are consumed. And some cause liver damage which is fatal and for which the only treatment is a liver transplant. Among wild mushrooms, he eats only gold-colored, trumpet-shaped chanterelles, and perhaps matsutakes with their clean pine scent, because he can identify them with certainty.

Our own parents exemplified the dangers of eating wild mushrooms. A friend whom they trusted to be an experienced forager gave them "chicken of the woods." They cooked it and ate it and both got such sudden and severe diarrhea that both bolted to the bathroom, but neither made it before they shat their pants.

On a hike in the Washington Cascades, I encountered several immigrants from Southeast Asia who were gathering mushrooms. They were sure that the plain white mushrooms they were collecting were the same as they had seen at home. I couldn't imagine a particular species travelling that far. I was terrified for their safety. The "Death Angel" grows around here. It is a big, plain white mushroom of the amanita family with a bulbous root and a shaggy ring around the stem where the cap pulls away from the stem as the mushroom grows. Befitting its name, it is deadly poisonous.

Common puffballs are supposed to be universally safe mushrooms. My college botany professor (back when mushrooms were thought to be plants) knew better. He picked, cooked, and ate puffballs and tossed some to his dog. He and the dog both got sick. He asked a multiple-choice question on our final exam, "How do you know that a mushroom is safe to eat?" The correct answer was, "You buy it in a can at Safeway."

I once saw a recipe box for sale at a craft show. It was a neat wooden box just the right size to hold 3 X 5 inch recipe cards. An artist had decorated it with hand-painted mush-rooms, not realizing I guess, that those bright red mush-rooms with white dots were deadly amanitas.

REFERENCES

Sheldrake, Merlin, *Entangled Life, How Fungi Make Our Worlds, Change Our Minds & Shape Our Futures*, New York, Random House (2020) Among other information, Sheldrake describes how shaped hyphae can be used as building or packing material.

Trudell, Steve, *Mushrooms of the Pacific Northwest: Timber Press Field Guide*. Portland, OR, 2d Edition 2022. I've heard Dr. Trudell say that he does not eat mushrooms, but only because he dislikes their texture.

CHAPTER 6

Lichens, Life's Little Mysteries

My husband likes to watch reruns of the TV series, "Stargate." It features a team of U.S. Air Force scientists and a friendly extra-terrestrial who explore worlds off Earth. Regularly the team encounters symbionts, two beings who share a body. Sometimes the symbiont who occupies a human body is evil, like Mr. Hyde when he dominates Dr. Jekyll in the Robert Louis Stevenson story. Sometimes the symbiont who shares a human body endows the human with special gifts — say, perfect pitch or the ability to understand all language — to benefit them both. (In reality, we human beings are symbionts. We are beginning to appreciate the gut bacteria that feed on the food we consume, whose secretions cross the blood-brain barrier to affect our moods, appetites, and mental health.)

Lichens are symbionts; they are fungi containing algae or cyanobacteria in strata within their fruiting bodies or mixed within their cells. The fungi provide a structure for their symbiotic algae or bacteria to adhere to a matrix where they both can grow, such as on garden soil, tree bark, or stones. The fungi hold to the substrate with hyphae (tissue that acts like roots) and bring nutrients to the algae or bacteria. In return, the algae or bacteria capture energy from sunlight, undergo photosynthesis, and generate sugars that they and the fungi can share.

I can see two types of lichens in my yard, each vastly different from the other. The first is a miniscule orange lichen that at first looks like nothing more than a flat orange stain on top of the concrete blocks of my retaining wall. Looking more closely, I see that it is comprised of raised dots so flat they are only slightly palpable, as though a pointillist painted them with a tiny brush. They colonize in circles, spreading out from a center like a drop of water splattering. In my yard, they stick to concrete, but I've seen them growing more thickly on tree bark.

My second lichen looks fancier. It is growing on a chunk of dark basalt stone that somebody once dumped over the embankment bordering my yard in a half-baked effort at landscaping. The rock tumbled to rest in an area that I have allowed to go wild. Now the rock rests beneath a Saskatoon shrub (Service Berry), somewhat shaded from intense afternoon sunlight coming in from the west. The lichen grows in a circle 3.5 inches across, greenish white at the edges, darker green at the center. It has leafy-looking parts called "thalli," crowded and overlapping, frilly at the edges, largely adhered to the rock, flapping freely only slightly at the edges.

I see round gray scars on the dark stone, perhaps where another lichen once grew. And I see new growths of it in smaller versions developing in spots on the rock.

I became more attentive to lichens when Seattle nature photographer Art Wolfe displayed a lovely close-up photograph depicting just the ruffled edge of a lichen.

These lichens, the crusty orange and the leafy circle, have proper Latin names. I can recognize them only as one of seven standard lichens classified by their shapes, with names like Snow White's Seven Dwarfs: Dusty, Crusty, Scaley, Leafy, Clubby, Shrubby, or Hairy. I could figure out maybe one or two more identifiers, like whether they are pigmented or not, whether they have a dead or mineral crust on their outer layer, whether they are wrinkled or warty, etc. But to identify them exactly requires at least a microscope to look at their cross-sections, chemical tests of their make-up, and ideally, tests of their DNA. Then I must realize that over 1,000 species have been identified in the Pacific Northwest so far.

Unable to be more specific, I'll simply acknowledge Crusty and Leafy in the yard.

REFERENCES

McCune, Bruce and Geiser, Linda, *Macrolichens of the Pacific Northwest, 2d. Ed.*, Corvallis, Oregon State University Press(2009.)

Pojar, Jim and MacKinnon, Andy, eds. *Plants of the Pacific Northwest Coast, Washington, Oregon, British Columbia and Alaska*, Vancouver, B.C. Lone Pine Publishing and B.C. Ministry of Forests (1994).

CHAPTER 7

Just Add Water — the Mosses

Our birdbath, a shallow basin on a pedestal, sits at the edge of a flower bed in my front yard. Birds use the bath daily and get it so filthy with dirt and droppings that it has to be hosed clean every day. Overspray lands on a patch of dirt about a foot square, and in my yard, that's where a thin skin of moss grows.

My backyard has a retaining wall constructed from concrete blocks with curved, rough front edges. Stacking the blocks brick style, with each block centered over the seam between two blocks on the tier below, creates a series of small shelves extending a few inches out from the wall. Dust blows in and a teaspoon or so of soil sifts from between the blocks, and that's enough to support moss.

I shouldn't expect to find moss in North Central Washington. Moss loves moisture, and our average rainfall is 7 inches per year. That meets the National Geographic's definition of a desert.

The kind of moss I find here looks and feels like clumps

of very short-napped green velvet. Magnifying it with a hand lens, I see a stem comprised of a stack of tiny, nested cups made of pointed leaves, each stem crowding shoulder to shoulder with its nextdoor neighbors. It sends up a thread about a ½ inch tall on top, finer than a human hair. Each thread is pale yellow with a spore capsule on top. When it dries, the entire moss turns into a crisp brown crust that looks too dead ever to revive. However, as soon as there is moisture, it springs back to life.

This moss is only a feeble reminder of the mosses that were familiar to me as a child. I grew up on the Oregon coast where our rainfall hit 100 inches annually. There, what we called "peat moss" could carpet the forest floor a foot deep. And on the wet west side of the Washington Cascade foothills, I've seen mosses that covered the arching limbs of vine maple, creating a green grotto. Moss coated the trunks of large-leafed maples so that they were Day-Glo green in the spring before the trees leafed out, while sunshine could still reach them.

Whenever I read one of Mary Oliver's poems in which she lies down in a meadow or in the forest to commune with nature and examine her life, I envision a bed of moss, and think, I wouldn't do that. I don't welcome invertebrates crawling on me, I don't want to crawl on them, either, and moss is loaded with them. Moss creates an insulated, damp habitat for them. Plenty, like centipedes, are easy to see. Plenty are microscopic.

From what I've read, moss is the normal habitat for tardigrades, "water bears," that, magnified, look to me like inflated paper bags with legs, claws, and a snout. It would take a powerful microscope for me to see the details of an animal the size of a period printed at the end of a sentence. They are extremophiles, so like the moss, they tolerate drying out. For me, the tardigrades symbolize the life that probably lies all around us, but which we humans just don't have the faculties to detect. But I'd be willing to bet that there are tardigrades in my yard, in the moss.

Before she became well known for her book *Braiding Sweetgrass,* Robin Wall Kimmerer wrote *Gathering Moss, a Natural and Cultural History of Mosses.* I think that the moss in my yard is what she calls a "City moss" because it survives in urban settings, growing on sidewalks, window ledges, and statues. My moss looks like the drawing of a cushion of *Gimmia pulvinate* in her book. On the other hand, *Plants of the Pacific Northwest Coast,* by Jim Pojar and Andy MacKinnon, describe something called "Red Roof Moss," *Ceratodon purpureus,* as the most common moss in the world, growing from New York sidewalks to the Antarctic. It would take a good microscope, more observation, and more experience for me to name the moss in my yard with any confidence. On the other hand, it's easy to understand how moss found its way into my yard. Kimmerer explains that mosses freeing their spores into the air create a cloud of "aerial plankton" that circulates around the entire globe, which undoubtedly would waft a few spores across this place.

REFERENCES

Kimmerer, Robin Wall: *Gathering Moss, A Natural and Cultural History of Mosses,* Corvallis, Oregon State University Press (2003)

National Geographic, https://www.nationalgeographic.com/environment/article/deserts

Pojar, Jim and MacKinnon, Andy, eds, *Plants of the Pacific Northwest Coast, Washington, Oregon, British Columbia and*

Alaska, Vancouver, B.C.; B.C. Ministry of Forests and Lone Pine Publishing (1994)

Acer circinatum: Vine maple

Acer macrophylum: Large-leafed maple

Ceratodon purpureus: Red roof moss

Gimmia pulvinate: a common "City moss."

Part III

Animals

CHAPTER 8

Assorted Invertebrates – Slugs, Sowbugs, Centipedes and Worms

As is the case with mosses–just add moisture. That's the sure-fire recipe for rousing the invertebrates that I've found in my yard. Because our environment is dry, I don't see many of them, but I'd be overlooking a major phyla of animals present in the yard if I didn't mention them.

Slugs

The slug is a snail that has lost its shell to evolution. It's possible to find slugs in my yard, but not often, and they are tiny gray, ¾ inch long models. They find perpetually damp habitats, like the bottoms of flowerpots sitting in an irrigated flower bed. They scarcely seem related to the 6 inch banana slugs of the wet side of the Cascades. Given their dependence on moisture to live, it's possible that they came into the yard on flowerpots and aren't native at all.

A former client of mine headed a laboratory that test-ed substances for pharmaceutical properties, working as a contractor for Big Pharma. I told him that somebody should test slug slime to understand just how persistently it can stick to skin. It won't wash off and it collects dirt. Couldn't it be a matrix for medicinal lotions? Could it keep moisture on a wound where that would be useful? "I'm sure they're working on it," he told me.

Unlike my desert yard, my childhood home on the Ore-gon coast supported a wealth of slugs, including big ones. In the garden, we always had to strip away the outermost leaves of the cabbages we grew because surely there would be a slug inside. The local hardware store sold boxes of slug bait (poison), and people shared folk lore that slugs would drown in a pan of beer set out to distract them from the garden (if you could keep your dog out of it; dogs love beer).

My nephew, who lives on the wet Oregon coast, pulled a classic kid stunt. "Mom, I have a science project due on Monday." That was about Thursday or Friday. With my sister's inspiration, he set up an experiment to test whether slugs really were attracted to beer. He set out three shal-low pans in the forest duff at the edge of their garden. He poured beer into one, half beer and half water into the sec-ond, and a quarter beer with three-quarters water into the third pan, and left them to the slugs overnight. His results were conclusive: Most slugs went for the undiluted beer, the half beer drew the second most, and the near beer drew the fewest. What was most remarkable was the raw num-ber. Most of the slugs were the tiny ones, and by the end of the weekend, they numbered in the hundreds.

Slugs are so rare here that I'm unlikely to sacrifice a per-fectly good beer to hunt for one.

Sowbug, Roly-Poly, Wood Lice

Sowbugs, pill bugs, roly-polys, or wood lice--whatever they're called, surely everybody has seen them. Sowbugs and pill bugs are crustaceans, like lobsters. They occupy the damp spots between the lawn and the sidewalk, under the flowerpots, or under scraps of lumber lying on the ground.

Actually, sowbugs and pill bugs aren't identical. If you disturb a sowbug, it runs away, waving its two-pronged tail-like appendage at you. A pill bug rolls into a ball behind the protection of its hard outer cover and has no tail to wave. They're likely to eat young lettuce seedlings, but they don't bite, sting, or even stink.

Centipedes

As a kid, I always heard that centipedes could sting or bite, although I never heard of anybody being hurt by one, and I'd seen plenty. On my damp Oregon coast, they were common in moss beds, under the bark of rotting windfallen trees, and under the firewood pile. Well, it turns out that the folklore is true!

Somehow, one got inside my house and climbed the bathroom wall. It was flat, reddish-brown, and had a pair of legs on each of its segments, providing plenty of legs for hanging onto the wall. I jumped back and left the room. Evidently it left by the same mysterious way it got in, because I didn't see it again. I did check some references that said their foremost legs have developed into fangs, they can bite enough to hurt, and they carry venom.

Folklore says that problems that go away by themselves come back by themselves, but so far, the centipede has not come back.

Earthworms

Which came first, rich soil or earthworms? Healthy soil contains plenty of organic matter. Earthworms like organic matter, so they like healthy soil. Turn over a clump of garden soil. If it's wormy, it's healthy. Worms make it healthier by grinding up and breaking down organic matter, concentrating its nutrients in its castings (fecal matter), and leave burrows that facilitate the flow of air and water through garden soil. I've read that worms can't tolerate the sun's rays. Because they are some of the good guys, if I uncover one, I immediately cover it back up.

In my yard, an American Robin plucks earthworms from the little patch of lawn but prefers to fill its beak with earthworms from the compost pile, where the hunting is easier.

With only one exception, the only worms I've found in the yard are pinkish earthworms, called angleworms if I impale them on a fishhook. I haven't found the larger pinkish worms with flattened tails that thrive in damp forest duff, "Nightcrawlers." The one exception was a worm as long as a nightcrawler, but round from end to end with no flattened tail like a nightcrawler, and as fat as a grub. I found it when I was turning over compost. It was pinkish except for bluish at the end of its tail. I covered it up quickly, but I had to wonder if it were one of the rare giant Palouse earthworms that have been discovered around here. To identify it, I would have to find one of the worm experts from the Palouse area in southeast Washington, where they were first located. Originally, they were described with more imagination than accuracy: Supposedly, they dug many feet deep, grew many feet long, and smelled like lilacs.

Earthworms have setae (like legs) to help them move, but they aren't conspicuous. Rather, the wriggling we see comes from muscles along their sides and a hydraulic sys-

tem that penetrates their body segments. It's such an inge-
nious mechanism that you could almost convince me that
it was an engineering team's intelligent design.

REFERENCES

Sampson, Susan Rae, "Too Rare To Be Endangered, the
Ironic Status of the Giant Palouse Earthworm Under the
Endangered Species Act," *Awake in the World,* Riverfeet
Press, 2017

CHAPTER 9

A Frog in the Throat?

I don't expect to find frogs in a desert; they love water. The body of water nearest my yard is an irrigation reservoir called "Lake Cortez" in the middle of our subdivision, about a quarter of a mile away. Frogs have found their way to Lake Cortez. Starting in March and running until sometime in June, I hear what sounds like a thousand voices calling "Ribbet ribbet ribbet ribbet," the song of tiny thumb-sized Pacific chorusing frogs, *Pseudacris regilla*. One story has it that movie soundtracks of chorusing frogs are this frog, no matter what the setting of the movie.

The frogs are familiar from my childhood on the Oregon coast. Mud puddles on our unpaved street became ponds that persisted until spring. Frogs would deposit jelly-like globs of eggs on the edges of the puddles, each with a dark spot in the center that would develop into a pollywog (or tadpole, the same thing). We'd scoop some up in a peanut butter jar, pond water and all, and watch them develop.

Here in the desert, we've had just one encounter with a frog within the bounds of our yard. One evening we heard the occasional hoarse croak of a frog, calling from somewhere near our deck. We couldn't get near enough to see it without its going quiet.

However, the next day, we spotted it. Jerry picked up a watering can that was sitting on the deck and tried to pour some water on a potted plant. The spout was plugged. Jerry inspected and found the frog completely inside the spout. It appeared to be a diurnal Cascades frog, about 2 inches across. It's a regular denizen of the nearby foothills and I'd seen it before on hikes. Jerry gently relocated it from the can to a flower bed near a dripper on the irrigation system.

Where there is one, no doubt there are more. It takes a whole population out there for there to be sightings at all. More than just Adam and Eve are required to sustain a population.

That's the problem I have with believing that the Sasquatch lives in the Cascades. If Sasquatches have been around for generations as stories contend, there have to be enough of them to sustain a population, and the sightings are too few and far between to suggest that there is a colony of them out there in the woods. Unless, of course, there is the Methuselah of a Sasquatch, a thousand-year-old, hiding out as effectively as D.B.Cooper.

REFERENCE:

https://savethefrogs.com/Pacific

CHAPTER 10

Snake!

As a kid, I wanted to see a rattlesnake. They don't appear on the soggy Oregon coast where I grew up. Somehow, I imagined that its fangs would be as substantial as those of a large dog, or maybe a tiger. The first one I ever saw was dead at a roadside rest area. I was surprised that its fangs were as fine as sewing needles.

We live in rattlesnake country. I've come across them while I was hiking in the nearby Cascade Foothills. The first time I heard their rattle noise, I knew what it was, and after that, I continued to jump whenever the wind rustled the dried leaves of the arrow leaf balsam root. When I saw a snake in person, "Keep away," Jerry warned me. "It's a little one, and they have the worst bite. They don't know how to mete out their venom, so they give you a full load."

Away from the foothills, I've seen them as roadkill, run over on the streets in our subdivision. They were near an undeveloped lot that the owner irrigated. No doubt the water attracted rodents and birds that were prey that attracted the snakes. The rattlesnakes have their imitators —

big, highly patterned gopher snakes inclined to sprawl across hiking paths and refusing to move. A rattlesnake would likelier slither away.

I did see a snake inside my yard. My raspberry patch was lush. The berry canes were as tall as I and close together. I dropped to my hands and knees and crawled under their canopy to inspect the irrigation drippers at their bases. There, stretched out no more than 12 inches in front of me, was the long body of a fat, highly patterned snake. It was so long that both ends were concealed by the raspberry plants—I couldn't check the tail for rattles, or the head for the distinctive triangular shape of a rattler. (I'd never purposely get close enough to see the tiny pits in its face that characterize it and other pit vipers anyway.) I crawled in reverse as fast as I could and stayed away.

Half an hour later, I heard the ever-present House Sparrows sounding their alarm call, but saw nothing. I wondered if my visitor had been a gopher snake—they are said to climb trees to go after birds' nests.

Official state websites minimize the odds of being bitten by a rattlesnake, but I have the allegedly rare experience of meeting three individuals who have been bitten by venomous snakes, at least one a rattler.

When I was still a teenager, I met a construction contractor who had come to town for a project that my father worked on. He told us about a job he'd worked on up the Umpqua River in Oregon. He heard a rattlesnake, but never saw it. He began to feel unwell, so left a foreman in charge and headed home early. At day's end when his crew knocked off work and were leaving the site, they passed his truck, pulled off to the side of the road, and saw him slumped over the steering wheel. They rushed him to a hospital. His doctors did not detect what was wrong until the lab tests came back. He had been bitten by a rattlesnake.

The second victim was my son, in Virginia. Seeing a snake under a picnic table where "old ladies" were gathering, he grabbed it behind the head to deposit it away from people. He left it with too much neck to maneuver, and it bit him in the finger. He had to be checked out in the ER and watched while his finger swelled to a big black blister. The snake was a copperhead; the doctor told him he was lucky — cottonmouth water moccasins, which are also endemic there, tend to cause infections beside being poisonous.

The third was my grandmother, in Florida. She was bitten while she worked in her garden. She never saw the snake. Her doctor could only say for sure that it wasn't a coral snake, or she would not have made it to the ER alive.

I regret it when I see snakes as roadkill in our neighborhood. It looks to me like they've been run over on purpose. That's unnecessary. We can live in perfect *détente*, like opponents in nuclear warfare, each equally too afraid of the other to take an aggressive action.

REFERENCE:

Washington Department of Wildlife website regarding rattlesnakes: https://wdfw.wa.gov/species-habitats/species/crotalus-oreganus

CHAPTER 11

Lounging Lizards

Every summer I see lizards in my yard. I was introduced to local lizards in a class I took from local naturalists.

The first I met in my own yard looked like a Northern Alligator Lizard. It does look exactly like a little alligator, with a long snout. However, my reference book says it grows 8 to 10 inches long, and the one I see in my yard is tiny, two inches long, basking on the concrete blocks of the wall that retains my garden. It's wary and skitters away if I make the slightest movement.

The other regular is a Western Fence Lizard. It is 6 inches long, and likes to climb, nothing better than a fence post, but a retaining wall or a pile of old bits of lumber will do. It sits ponderously, chinless, like Jabba the Hutt.

I suspect that the lizards dig deep into the garden soil, or dig in under my garden shed, to hibernate all win-ter. That's my impression after meeting a retired teacher whose students made a study of horny toads (technically, horned lizards). She taught at Waterville, a village across the Columbia River from us, up on the shrub-steppe plateau. Her students enlisted local farmers to record the latitude and longitude coordinates of where they saw horned lizards while they plowed their wheat fields. The students caught some lizards and put them in a pen to watch them dig in for the winter. They put a screen in the soil 18 inches beneath the surface of the pen so that the lizards would not dig their way out. But when spring came, the lizards did not reappear. The students excavated the pen and found the remains of their lizards 18 inches down, where they had been blocked by the screen from digging any further.

That was sad, but they did achieve some citizen science. They documented the presence of horned lizards in north central Washington; and they proved that the lizards would dig deeper than 18 inches into the earth, and had to go deeper, to winter over.

REFERENCE

Mathews, Daniel, *Cascade-Olympic Natural History, A Trailside Reference*, Portland: Raven Editions and Portland Audubon Society, 1988.

CHAPTER 12

My Life With Insects

I have consciously interacted with insects in minor ways my whole life. I suspect the same is true for billions of people.

Insects have been my playthings. As a kid, I bounded through the backyard after grasshoppers, and if I caught one, I let it "spit tobacco" on my hands—it exuded a brown liquid from its mouth. Early summer brings out tiny grasshopper nymphs that look like adults, but that grow quickly and molt their old exoskeletons, developing bigger and bigger sets of armor, so that by July the ½ inch cuties are now full-sized brown flyers over 2 inches long. They chomp their way through the garden, leaving ragged holes in leaves. At least they are too few to eat very much. In *The Worst Hard Time*, Timothy Egan documents the plague of grasshoppers that hit the dust bowl during the 1930s, eating every shred of vegetation, then the clothing on the clothesline and the leather harnesses on horses.

Edith Shiffert wrote a string of poems with forms inspired by Japanese haikus and tankas. She wrote "Grasshopper":

> On cliff-top grasses too
>
> a grasshopper
>
> with goggle eyes
>
> and knees bent backwards
>
> existing.

If I found another playmate, a ladybug, I recited, "Ladybug, Ladybug, fly away home, your house is on fire and your children are alone." That nursery rhyme dates back to 1744 and has some versions that rhyme better.

I turned click beetles over onto their backs, then watched and listened as they jerked their heads, propelling themselves into the air with an audible click, flipping themselves right-side up.

I spent a warm spring day on the banks of the Coos River in Oregon letting mosquitoes bite my arm. I watched each biter's abdomen swell with blood, then I slapped it! I covered my arm with gore.

My friend Merry told me that if I'd pulled my skin taut while the mosquito was still sucking on me, it would get stuck and drink until it exploded.

Another friend, Mark, spent summers in the interior of Alaska, where the mosquito was named the state bird. He told of people allowing the mosquitoes to bite, then slapping them once and counting the bodies. I recalled that European fairy tale about "Seven with one blow." That braggart was a duffer by Alaska standard. The record was over 100.

By late summer, the praying mantis cracks out of its cocoon. Three cocoons are stuck to the underside of a handrail in my garden right now. They are greenish tan, 1.25 inches long, and look like slugs from any distance, but have a ringed texture that's visible up close. I tried to catch a fat adult by scooping it into a jelly jar for a closer look, but it pinched me, hard, and I let it go. Once pinched, twice shy — I'll get my closer look out of a book.

I'm aware of the cricket in the yard because of the continuous buzzing noise it makes; and it must be aware of me, by my noise, or smell, or looming presence (relative to its size), because as soon as I try to track it down, it stops its music. One evening, I was contented just to listen to it strum, and wrote about it:

One Cricket

Summer fizzles out like an ember,

corn stalks are yellow and tall,

yet nights remain hot.

After dark, one cricket strums

where a whole choir joined him

before.

Perhaps he's like Aesop's grasshopper

who blithely played on

while ants labored,

but what do I know about

insects' lives?

Maybe this cricket

is the star performer

to whom the others listen in awe

the greatest solo artist ever,

the Yo-Yo Ma

of the insect world.

Every day I meet a large variety of insects in my garden. When I mow, a cloud of thrips arises from the grass. Bees and flies fly in clouds around the blooming flowers. Beetles scamper under the cover of scrap lumber. Midges hover in flecks of light. Most are old friends who won't alarm me; rationally, none should horrify me. Yet, when I check their sizes according to the scale in my bug book, I am surprised how much smaller they are, compared to how large I perceive them to be.

I read once that if all matter on Earth became invisible except for insects, we would still see the outline of every structure on the planet, because it would still be outlined by the insects that populate our environment so thickly. I would be interested in seeing my garden that way, although only for a few minutes. Any longer, I might be horrified.

I have identified many of the insects in my yard only at the family level; genus and species will have to await a better bug catcher and another day.

Click Beetles: *Elaterodae*

Crickets: *Grillidae*

Grasshoppers: *Acrididae*

Lady Bugs, Lady Beetles. *Coccinellidae.* I've seen *Cycloneda polit, the* Western Blood-red Lady Beetle in my yard. Yes, I count the spots on the backs of the red ones to identify their species.

Mosquitoes: *Culicidae*

Yellow jackets and paper wasps: *Vespidae*. Romantics know that the Vespa, the wasp, is the Italian motor scooter that Gregory Peck and Audrey Hepburn use to buzz through Rome's traffic in the 1953 movie *Roman Holiday*.

REFERENCES

Egan, Timothy: *The Worst Hard Time, The Untold Story of Those Who Survived the Great American Dust Bowl*, Boston and New York, Houghton Mifflin Company (2006)

Peterson, Merrill A.: *Pacific Northwest Insects*, Seattle, Seattle Audubon Society 2018

Shiffert, Edith: *New and Collected Poems*, Buffalo, N.Y., White Pine Press (1979)

CHAPTER 13

Pismires, Pisants, Pissants, and Ants

The ants in my yard annoy me, astonish me, and clean up messes for me.

Little black ants annoy me when spring warms up the walls on the south and west sides of the house and they decide to come inside. The ants who want to be inside are only one tenth of an inch long, too tiny to be deterred by a screen door. They will enter the walls of the house and emerge out of the electrical outlet boxes. Their common name is "odorous house ant" and their proper name is *Tapinoma sessile,* but some people call them "sugar ants" because they do find the kitchen and they do get into the food.

My son Eric had an unpleasant experience with sugar ants. At the time, he usually drove an SUV with three rows of seats, chauffeuring his three sons and often a couple of their friends to their school, sports, and social events. The boys snacked in the car and dribbled their treats. When Eric and I used the vehicle to haul some yard furniture, we dropped the tailgate and uncovered a colony of sugar ants, thriving on the dregs of Oreos and the drips of smoothies.

The ants that astonished me were reddish brown and looked larger to me than sugar ants. I was walking through the backyard when I caught movement out of the corner of my eye. I thought that I'd seen a stick that was crawling in the yard. When I investigated, I saw a crowd of ants moving in a column several feet long. They crossed a gravel path, climbed 12 inches to the top of the retaining wall, crossed the flower bed at the top of the wall, marched through the chain link fence, and disappeared into the undeveloped, weedy lot next door. It's possible they were "pavement ants," *Tetramorium* species. That species is known to swarm on sidewalks, but I've also seen them in other places. On a hot summer day, the ants emerged from under the steppingstones in my front yard and covered the stones with themselves and their eggs.

The ants that cleaned up a mess were black ants. Some animal, a cat or a racoon, had dumped feces on the patio, and in the evening when I noticed it, ants were swarming over it. I let them be. By morning, the mess was completely gone.

I call them sugar ants or odorous ants, but in archaic English, ants were called "pismires," then "pisants." Those terms derived from "piss" because of their formic acid odor. In America, by the early 1900s, a "pissant" was a detestable person, as bad as our politicians' "deplorables" today, and the term has found its way into many languages.

REFERENCE

Peterson, Merrill A.: *Pacific Northwest Insects,* Seattle, Seattle Audubon Society (2018)

CHAPTER 14

The Working Animals – Bees and Flies

Bees and flies, like police dogs and dairy cows, are the working animals in my neighborhood. My subdivision sits amid commercial orchards producing apples, cherries, pears, and apricots. European Honeybees and other flies and bees pollinate those crops. Beekeepers rent out their hives to fruit growers, delivering them into the orchards in bloom. Meanwhile, the beekeepers' competitors are salesmen who call on orchardists, pressuring them to buy pollen to apply artificially before supplies run out. I overheard one salesman doing just that, buttonholing a potential customer in the lobby of the local post office.

My nearby neighbors have an orchard and their own European honeybees. The bees occupy an old shed on their property and have nested there since the 1950s. Every once in a while, the colony generates a new swarm, and my neighbor has to capture them and carry them at least three miles away. He says that if he releases them closer, they will fly home. He drives them to his brother's ranch about 10 miles away. He says he'd like to get rid of their old shed, but he won't, so long as the bees find a home there. He can glance at the bee shed to see whether the daytime temperature has reached 55 degrees F. The bees won't come outside until they are warm enough.

Some European Honeybees get distracted from their orchards and work a side gig in my yard. Many more pollinating species work here, too. The big, fuzzy, bumblebee (*Bombus*) comes to mind, but I've read alarming reports that the whole genus is diminishing rapidly.

Douglas Tallamy, PhD, the naturalist who calls for planting native flora to attract native fauna to our yards, recommended planting a roll of toilet paper in the ground to invite bumblebees to use for a nest. That's a sweet idea, but when store closures due to the Covid-19 pandemic took effect, retailers saw a run on toilet paper. For fear of running out, I didn't want to sacrifice a whole roll, so I planted a roll that was two-thirds empty. I put it in a quiet, dry, sunny place in my berry patch. I hoped no neighbors were watching. Would they think I was burying toilet paper because it was precious, like a miser hiding his gold? As far as I can tell, no bee has even looked at it.

Then I learned that what I thought was a bumblebee actually was not; judging from photos and the dark spot in the middle of its fuzzy yellow thorax, I'd seen a bumblebee-mimic, *Anthophora*. I saw another look-alike that turned out to be a big, fuzzy, brown and yellow flower fly (*Eristolis flavipes*) with a rust-colored stripe across its abdomen, and not a bee at all.

I found sweat bees (Halictidae family) when I noticed little sand volcanoes in the yard. Big eyes on short bodies peered out, then bees emerged, one per hole, flashing bright metallic red or green bodies.

Tiny flying insects love the plants in my yard that have tiny flowers. They hover around their favorites, darting in and out too fast for me to see them clearly, then spend several seconds on a flower before darting into the air again. They prefer the umbelliferous plants, those tall stems having flat flowers arrayed in spokes on top, supporting miniscule blossoms. In my yard, the umbelliferous plants include dill, fennel, and Italian parsley.

One of my tiny flyers might be the mason bee. Mason bees (*Megachilidae* family) are three-tenths of an inch long. The probability is very high that I've seen them here, since about 200 different species of mason bees alone live across the Pacific Northwest. However, I don't plan to capture them to place them under a microscope to count the number of teeth in their mandibles just for the sake of a firm identification. (Either a zealot or a scientist determined, for example, that one mason bee, *Hoplitis hypocrite,* has three teeth per mandible.)

Friends on Facebook advocate building habitats to support mason bees, such as leaving stacks of small tubes or wood blocks drilled full of holes in warm places in the yard for them to nest. But I wonder how dedicated my friends will be about caring for their mason bees when it's time to rinse their nests of mites before their larvae winter over. Oregon State University publishes instructions online for doing that.

Another tiny flier in my yard is the hover fly (*Syrphidae* family). It is just as tiny and quick as a mason bee and can be striped black and yellow, like some bees; there are 400 species of them in the Pacific Northwest. Both mason bees and hover flies are marvelous pollinators.

Bee or fly? The big giveaway is the number of their wings. Bees have four wings, flies have two. (All flies are *diptera*. The "di" means "two;" the ptera means "wing.")

Bees or flies, no matter what we call them, are hard-working insects busy performing ecological services as pollinators. The little ones demonstrate that I don't have to feel repugnant toward all flies just because fat green bottle flies crawl on dung. Because both the little bees and flies seem abundant, and because both are great pollinators, they give me hope that effects of the colony collapse among European honeybees in recent years can be overcome.

Recently I've learned about some hobbyist beekeepers who call themselves "Natural beekeepers." They blame commercial beekeepers for the collapse of their hives. "Parasites, pathogens, poor nutrition, and pesticides," they complain. The mite *Varoa destructer* is the parasite. Hives are placed too close together so that pathogens can spread more easily among them. The bees suffer poor nutrition because the keepers gather too much of their food and beeswax, leaving too little for hives to winter over. Colonies should be smaller like their sizes in the wild. Colonies should be allowed to swarm, leaving mite eggs behind. Hives should be hung high in trees and as far apart as they would be found in nature, they contend. These hobbyists are the organic farmers of beekeeping, and admittedly they sustain a cost for "doing it right." However, since 90% of American beekeepers are hobbyists with twenty or fewer hives, they don't need to be so productive. That's not how they earn their livings.

Maybe the orchardists can take lessons from the natural beekeepers, since they aren't producing honey for commerce, either. Then, perhaps they can foster more species in their orchards, like hover flies, and like mason bees with their tube nests freshly scrubbed of mites.

REFERENCE

Knight, Sam: "Hive Mind, is beekeeping wrong?" *The New Yorker*, August 28, 2023

Peterson, Merrill A.: *Pacific Northwest Insects*, Seattle, Seattle Audubon Society 2018

CHAPTER 15

Butterflies

Folk etymology says that "butterfly" comes from "flutter by;" that's charming, but erroneous. The term comes from *"buterfleoge,"* an old English term derived from German, where the name would sound more like "booter flooga."

During the summer, I see only a few species of butterflies making daily visits to my yard. Many other species of butterflies and moths are endemic here, but I'm not seeing them. I've seen pretty Admirals and Mourning Cloaks, and tiny blue butterflies, the latter settling on mud, during my hikes in the Cascade Foothills, but not in my garden. Just how much I was missing came home to me on a class field trip to Blewett Pass several years ago. Our guest leader was Robert Michael Pyle, author of *Butterflies of Cascadia*. Our class had walked the same route at least twice in recent weeks without seeing the many species he spotted and brought to our attention.

Dr. Pyle demonstrated how to sneak up behind a butter-fly, net the insect, then quickly twist the net shut so the insect couldn't escape. He moved spryly for a man who was in his late 60s, also my age at the time. He enticed a butterfly to land on his hand, then placed it on a classmate's nose, where the insect was happy to perch and sip salt from her skin for several minutes. Pyle assured us that the butterflies he caught that day were not at all endangered, so we did no harm by capturing a few. He is a founder of the Xerxes Society, which works for preservation of invertebrate habitats, so I guess if he says it's okay to catch a few, it's okay.

Dr. Pyle is a polymath. He writes poetry and essays. Another classmate was much more interested in Dr. Pyle's book about the Sasquatch rather than butterflies, so I gave him my copy of Dr. Pyle's book, *Where Bigfoot Walks*. When I met him, Dr. Pyle was cultivating a reputation as a character. He had given his butterfly net a name, Marsha. After our field trip, he sold some of his books from the trunk of a notably battered old car.

Of the butterflies I do see within my yard, the first are cabbage moths, a plain white-winged insect with just a simple black dot and a black edge on its front wings. *Pieris rapae* is a little short of an inch long. I see a pair of them circling one another, dancing a do-si-do in four dimensions. And true to their name, they are pests on cabbage plants. The way my mother cursed that insect, I halfway expected to see her sitting at the edge of her garden with a shotgun across her lap, ready to turn exterminator.

I don't grow cabbages, so in my yard, cabbage moths just flit around looking for absolutely anything else to eat, ideally something from the mustard family, like teenagers raiding the refrigerator.

Watching their erratic route, I am reminded of a children's story in which a Native American Indian boy tells another child that he learned to move quickly by chasing butterflies. The other child is insulted, thinking the Indian is lying, but he's telling the truth.

My second visitor is the big, showy western tiger swallowtail butterfly, with a body 1.6 to 2 inches long. It has yellow wings with black edges and black tiger stripes running from the front of its wing back through the yellow. The trailing edge of the wing is dotted with yellow, and blue and red dots near the base of its two swallow tails. Its wings are showy and so is its body–it is bright yellow, like a dancer in a leotard. It seems to call regularly right around noon. It flits the length of the flower garden, flying high and low, crossing against the wind effortlessly, examining roses and wild showy milkweed. It finds something it likes and keeps coming back for more.

I've allowed the wild showy milkweed to occupy a corner of the yard because that plant feeds monarch butterflies. In fact, milkweed is necessary for survival of the monarch. No monarchs are likely to come through, though; they have always been rare in this range. The huge loss of habitat due to wildfires along their migration route in Northern California is likely to make their visits even rarer. But the showy milkweed is pretty, not difficult to pull out when it spreads, and along with zinnias, the swallowtail likes it.

P.S. While I was writing this chapter, I took a day off to visit the Cassimer Bar Natural Area at the confluence of the Okanogan and Columbia Rivers, about a 60 mile drive northeast of home. No sooner had I stepped from my car than I saw a monarch butterfly. I photographed it, checked the I.D. with Dr. Pyle's book, and confirmed it with a friend who is a monarch aficionado. He connected me with the Western Monarch Milkweed Mapper, a website supported by Washington and Idaho Fish and Game Departments and the Xerces Society. They had me upload my photo and the details of the sighting to their website. I am now represented by a data point.

REFERENCE

Pyle, Robert Michael: *The Butterflies of Cascadia,* The Audubon Society, Seattle (2002)

Pyle, Robert Michael: *Where Bigfoot Walks: Crossing the Dark Divide*, originally published by Houghton Mifflin of New York and Boston; now published by Counterpoint Press, Berkley (1995)

Western Monarch Milkweed Mapper, https://www.monarchmilkweedmapper.org/

CHAPTER 16

Ornery Yellowjackets

None of my reference books or anything I've read attributes a personality to a wasp or a yellowjacket, but I have an opinion. I think they are aggressive, angry, and malicious.

I have seen paper wasps living in colonies in the paper-mâché balloons they've made from chewed-up wood and plants and hung in trees. I've seen them pasting a handful of open-bottomed cells onto the eave soffits of my house. I've seen the yellowjackets nesting in small groups in the forest soil and in crevices in a rockery. Seeing their different lifestyles indicates that I'm seeing three different species, and a quick glance at a reference book shows me that many more look much the same.

As kids, we always warned one another that yellowjackets could sting more than once because, unlike honeybees, they didn't lose their stingers by attacking. It's true I've never had to pull out one of their stingers, but it's also true that once stung, I've slapped, swatted, and run away rather than give it another stab at me.

Aggressive? I've had them drive me away from a picnic because they came after my food, especially the protein, so aggressively. I couldn't spray them away — who wants to eat fried chicken seasoned with DEET?

Malicious? I've been nailed by a ground-dwelling yellowjacket in the deep forest in autumn while I was foraging for mushrooms. It didn't give me a warning buzz. I didn't even see it until I felt the sting, then saw it flying away. A fleck of sunlight highlighted its yellow colors against the backdrop of the gloomy forest. It was pretty, actually, in its classical wasp pose, dangling its long legs as it flew.

Angry? When I lived in Seattle, yellowjackets moved into a hole in the rockery beside my driveway. I'd see them every time I drove in or out. Two yellowjackets always stood guard, one at each side of the entry to their hole. They looked like bouncers at a celebrity nightclub.

Today, a plethora of yellowjackets occupy my yard, especially in the warm seasons. There is always a handful of them sipping water from the birdbath, like tipplers at a bar. They work as pollinators alongside the honeybees, mason bees, and hover flies, and I'm grateful for that. Still, I patrol the eaves to knock down the wasps nests. They are just too ornery for me to feel safe when they build too close to the door.

REFERENCE

Peterson, Merrill A.: *Pacific Northwest Insects,* Seattle, Seattle Audubon Society (2018)

CHAPTER 17

Specialists

Some of the insects I see in my yard are specialists. Unlike a bee that might visit the oregano, the roses, and the berry flowers, the specialists live on precisely one species and nothing else. I've found at least three such specialists in my yard. What's amazing to me is that they've all found their perfect homes here.

The first specialist I found was the red-femured milkweed borer. It's a small rectangular beetle, about 1/3 of an inch to 3/4 of an inch long. It is showy bright red with a few black spots on its elytra, the thickened, hardened front wings that cap its rear wings and legs, as in most beetles. It has long black-and-white striped antennae. It lives on the wild showy milkweed that I've allowed to come up in my yard. My insect book, *Pacific Northwest Insects,* says that its larvae live within the stems and roots of the milkweed, then the adults feed on the flowers and leaves.

Wild showy milkweed is pretty, but invasive. I've let it come up in a patch in my yard to help feed monarch butterflies should any happen to fly through, but they are rare around here, so instead of monarchs, the milkweed has attracted orange-colored aphids and that red milkweed borer.

The borer is a wary insect. When I try to sneak close enough to take a photograph, it sees me and flies away to another nearby plant.

As far as I can tell, both the milkweed and the red-femured milkweed beetle are Northwest natives. The showy milkweed probably arrived as a wind-blown seed since I saw no other source for it in my neighborhood when it first appeared. (I notice that a neighbor has a patch growing in her yard downwind from me. I hope she doesn't mind.) Somehow, that particular beetle located that particular flower.

The second specialist I've encountered is the *Diplolepis* wasp — probably. I can't say for certain that I have laid eyes on her. Peterson's book says she is "small" and "hunch-backed." I might have mistaken her for some sort of flying ant. Her photograph shows a black insect with an ovoid head like an ant's, and reports that 750 species live in North America, seventy-five of which can be found in the Pacific Northwest. She causes galls to develop on my eglantine rose.

"*Diplolepis*" is her genus; I can't identify her down to a species, but possibilities include *D. rosea* and *D. bicolor,* both of which cause galls. Another species is named *D. eglanteria,* and since eglantine is the plant she affects in my yard, so I suspect she's the culprit. When the wasp meets the rose, she deposits her eggs into its stem. The rose reacts by developing a gall that looks like a ball of moss the size of a golf ball where wasp larvae hatch.

Eglantine, *Rosa rubinosa,* also called sweetbriar, is a shrub with hooked thorns and six-foot long branches that spring from a central root mass. The branches arch like spray from a fountain. In the spring, the rose develops an incon-spicuous five-petaled flower one inch across, having no fragrance. What is attractive about eglantine is the aroma of its leaves. In warm, wet weather, they smell like green apples.

Diplolepis is native, but eglantine is not. It comes from Europe and western Asia. It is a popular hedgerow plant in Britain. Eglantine rose was said to be a favorite of Queen Elizabeth I, whose portrait was often decorated with both the Tudor rose and eglantine.

Shakespeare mentioned eglantine in his popular poem from *A Midsummer Night's Dream:*

I know a bank where the wild thyme blows,

Where oxlips and nodding violets grow,

Quite over canopied with luscious woodbine,

With sweet musk rose and with eglantine.

The wasp has my eglantine plant hung all over with win-ter-killed brown galls like decorations on a dead Christ-mas tree.

I bought that rose from an internet source and planted it in a corner of my yard. For years, it had no galls, so I don't think I brought in the wasp with the plant. Now, even cut-ting the plant back severely does not save it from infesta-tion. The other roses in my garden are not affected. I've never seen another eglantine growing anywhere on this dry side of the Cascade Mountains, so what amazes me is that this specific wasp found this specific rose.

Wait a minute, my entomologist friend warns. It seems unlikely that the wasp could have evolved to favor eglan-tine in the mere 500 years or so since human immigrants brought it from England. On the other hand, since 750 species of wasps live in North America alone, I wonder if they don't mutate and evolve relatively quickly and successfully, compared to other insects. Only beetles seem to have speciated more widely.

The third specialist insect I've seen in my yard is the hollyhock weevil, *Rhopalapion longirostre*. It is miniscule, only about 1/5 of an inch long, with a gray elytrum and orange legs and a long snout sticking out in front. It is not native to the Pacific Northwest.

Like the weevil, the hollyhock (*Alcea rosea*) is an immigrant. Hollyhocks are so popular and so widespread that they seem like old-fashioned pioneer flowers, but they are natives of Europe and Asia. Their stalks, often six feet tall or taller, are studded with flowers in the shape of teacups tipped on their sides, spilling yellow pollen on petals that may be maroon, red, pink, white, or yellow. They are biannual, growing leaves their first year, blooming their second year, then shedding copious amounts of seed and dying back. A piece of its root might branch off and start a new shoot.

I read in a seed catalogue that before indoor plumbing was widespread, a row of hollyhocks marked the location of an outhouse.

I spotted hollyhock weevils when I noticed something was harming the fresh tips of their stalks, so I looked closely. The weevils were hanging out with their friends, clustering on tender new growth and piecing it with their typical weevil proboscises. Having heard of insects named for plants, like the red milkweed beetle or the box elder bug, I thought I was being facetious when I called them hollyhock weevils. That, I learned, truly was their common name.

So what I want to know is how did that beetle, not from around here, find that flower, not from around here, and do so at exactly the right time to take up residence in the new plant. My entomologist friend answers, "The short and superficial answer is almost certainly via olfaction." We smell the plants; their aromas are volatile, and bugs smell them, too.

He adds, "But your question could be a mind map of ramifying questions, from sensory biology to population dynamics to biogeography." He sees a master's thesis or doctoral dissertations arising out of my inquiry. "With six years of research, you would have an answer."

Resources

Peterson, Merrill A: *Pacific Northwest Insects,* Seattle Audubon Society (2018)

CHAPTER 18

True Bugs

There's true love. There's true north. And there are true bugs. All true bugs are insects that have mouth parts built for piercing.

In my yard, the most numerous true bugs are aphids, that plethora of tiny insects that can coat a tender flower part like a blanket. Sometimes they infect my pink Perfume Delight rose, and I wash them off. Mostly, I see bright orange aphids completely covering the underside of the leaves of the wild showy milkweed. I'm told that the bright color is a warning to predators that they taste nasty, like the orange monarch butterfly that feeds on milkweed. I don't have monarchs here, just matching orange aphids.

I've seen a boxelder bug, which is a true bug, warming itself in the overhang of the siding on the house. My entomologist friend assures me that it is harmless to the siding.

I found what I'm fairly sure was a western conifer seed bug (*Leptoglossus occidentalis*), even though they are usually found in forests. My neighbor's eight large ponderosa pines might have harbored it. What surprised me was that when it flew away, I heard it making a buzzing noise.

The final true bug I've encountered in the yard is the green stink bug, *Chinavia hilaris*. It is shaped like a shield, an oval with a slightly flattened top set with a half-circle head, the bottom rounded. It's small, only 2/5 to 7/10 of an inch long. And true to its name, it stinks. When I accidentally brush one in my berry patch, it puts out an odor that is substantial for such a small bug.

There are no words in the English language that I can use to recreate the odor of a stink bug so that anybody else could perceive it. It isn't putrid or musty or chemical; it's acrid, vegetative, bitter, rank. Smelling a stink bug is like hearing a rattlesnake or seeing a barracuda for the first time—or like true love—when it happens, you just know it.

REFEENCE

Peterson, Merrill A.: *Pacific Northwest Insects,* Seattle, Seattle Audubon Society (2018)

CHAPTER 19

Spiders

Of all the creatures in my yard, none has inspired so much mythology as the order of spiders, from the class of arachnids.

For the ancient Greeks, Arachne was a skillful weaver who challenged the goddess Athena to a weaving contest. Athena wove a tapestry glorifying the gods. Arachne wove a tapestry that depicted the foibles of the gods, disparaging them. Athena was angry, but rather than kill Arachne, allowed her to live on as a spider, to weave forever.

For the Hopi people of the American Southwest, Spider Grandmother taught human beings how to weave and how to make pottery. In Ghana, the spider is Anansi, a trickster, whose stories came to the western hemisphere with enslaved people, then spread throughout the Caribbean. In Japan, Tsuchigumo is depicted as a giant spider whom heroes seek to destroy.

Judging by the number of webs I see, I believe my yard contains a generous array of spiders. They drape sheets of webbing over the branches of the arbor vitae hedge. The sheets are so thin and translucent that they are practically invisible until they are decorated with dew or dust. The wind catches longer strands and spins them into strings filled with dust, leaf fragments, and small feathers. The American Goldfinch gathers the strands and drags them away to help build its nest. In contrast to the smooth sheets of webbing, messy, disorganized cobwebs fill corners of our deck, and an orb weaver decorates a tomato plant with a circular composition as broad across as a dinner plate.

Of all the spiders, there are only three that I can identify with any certainty. One is the crab spider — more precisely, the goldenrod crab spider, *Misumina vatia*. It is tiny, the female's body running 2/10 to 3/10 of an inch long. It's twice the size of the male. It rests in flowers and matches their color — white, yellowish, or greenish, with a red stripe running down the sides of its abdomen. It has eight conspicuous eyes set in two rows of four across its face. What makes it a "crab spider" is its flat body and the stance it takes, with its two front legs held out in front and turned slightly toward one another, ready to grab its prey. It looks exactly like a miniature Dungeness crab.

Easily the prettiest spider I've seen in the yard is the Cross Orb Weaver, *Araneus diadematus*. It is reddish-brown with striped legs befitting Pippi Longstocking and is decorated with a white St. Andrew's cross on its upper side. The cross is a big "X", signifying the martyr St. Andrew being crucified with his arms held aloft and legs apart. Stripes cross the spider's body on the underside. I saw it when it built an orb web suspended vertically on one of my tomato plants. What caught my attention was not only the presence of its orbits, but the shape of the radii in the web. They weren't straight. They zig-zagged like something Picasso would have drawn. I watched it daily for over a week, until time or the wind or a predator took it down.

And I recognize our Black Widows. The female is glossy black and has a round hump of an abdomen. Her body is over 1/2 an inch long, and with her long legs, she can grow to a noticeable 1-1/2 inches. The male is smaller and less spectacular. The first I saw was walking steadily down the road like a spider on a mission. I observed, then went home to check references to see if indeed I had seen a black widow. The second one I saw was just remains, a mummy hanging in a corner of our garage. Jerry doubted me, but checked for himself, then agreed. Then he saw a live one in the garage near a freezer. We pulled the freezer away from the wall, but didn't find it, so we decided that we would co-exist peacefully, with due regard for her space.

The Cross Orb Weaver Spider

The spider that has woven an orbital web

on the edge of my tomato patch

It's called a "Cross Orb Weaver,"

for the brown pattern on its yellow back.

My garden is a productive site for the spider--

Its web is studded with its mummified flies.

It fixes the slightest tears in its lines

with perfectly zig-zagged stitches of silk.

I try not to disturb its guy-lines

when I harvest the garden fruit.

But the spider has erred

in tying its web to plants.

Tomato plants are ephemeral,

they don't last.
Sooner or later I'll pull them out
after I've gathered their final fruit,
or else they will blacken and collapse
with the first hard frost.
The spider will be like the man
who built his house on a tract of sand
and suffered a great fall.

CHAPTER 20

Wild Animal Wars

Located as it is between the Cascade Foothills and the Columbia River, amid orchards, our subdivision overlaps the historical territories of deer, coyotes, rabbits, bats, and raccoons.

We see the bats flitting through our airspace at dusk, flying in jerky patterns after airborne insects. Enough trees surround us to provide them with hidden habitat so that they don't try to nest in our eaves.

A local naturalist told me that a bat's only sound, used for echolocation, is supersonic, but I know better. When the asphalt siding on my uncle's house buckled, bats moved into the shelter behind the bulges. As kids, we'd pound on the side of the house to hear the bats squeal.

When my mother moved into an assisted living facility, her house stood empty. So many bats moved into her chimney that I could hear them from the driveway when I drove up to inspect her place. I had planned to spend the night there; I drove off and rented a motel room.

The problem with bats is that they carry rabies. When I worked for the City of Seattle, one of my occasional coffee-break companions had an unpleasant encounter with bats. They invaded his house, and because they carry rabies, he and his family had to undergo precautionary rabies treatment.

(Speaking of rabies, when a neighbor's dog escaped his yard and bit me, Animal Control required the neighbor to impound the dog indoors for ten days to rule out illness. Afterwards, the dogcatcher called me and said, "If you're foaming at the mouth, it's not the dog's fault.")

Bears and cougars keep farther away, and the marmots tend to stay in their rock piles.

It isn't often, but we see deer wandering through the neighbor's apple orchard. We see coyotes loping through the golf course beyond the orchard, although they are definitely more heard than seen. They yip during their autumn breeding season, and during the summer when their pups are hungry, they sound like a thousand voices howling from the hillsides.

It's the raccoons who make themselves right at home. My war with raccoons sounds like a tall tale that Uncle Buck used to tell, so imagine I am telling you this with a western twang in my voice.

It started with a sewage smell we detected when we used the deck that surrounds the south and west sides of the house. We keep our septic tanks pumped; I assumed we had negligent neighbors. But then we caught sight of plump, fuzzy raccoons moving through the yard. The space beneath the deck wasn't large enough for me to crawl in to inspect, so I sprawled on the ground, shined a powerful flashlight under the deck, and used my binoculars.

I was horrified to see a huge pile of poop studded with

cherry seeds. My husband installed a critter cam, and in short order, we saw that raccoons, indeed, were using that space.

We did whatever any red-blooded American couple would do—we checked online to see if the government would help. Chelan County and local animal control were clear—they do not deal with wildlife, especially raccoons.

They referred us to the State Department of Fish and Wildlife. We did not call. We could imagine a State SWAT team coming in to trap our visitors and to eliminate them with "extreme prejudice" or to relocate them at taxpayer expense. I don't know about raccoons, but not all animals can be relocated. The wild animal that has been most successful in moving into cities, besides the raccoon, is the coyote. My friend Rick Kieffer, a retired chief of police, had to look into relocating coyotes for his city, the City of Normandy Park. The issue arose when coyotes started confronting pets on leashes while their owners walked little Fifi or Muffy. But if a coyote is relocated and is placed into an area already marked by another coyote, its chances of survival are poor. Back home in Malaga, we decided to look into self-help.

Now, a raccoon is just about the cutest animal you can imagine. It wears a black mask across its face, it has fluffy fur and a fluffy striped tail, it is smart, and it has exquisitely dexterous hands that it can use to open doors and tear into bags of cat food. I've seen a mama raccoon holding back her babies like a human mother cautious about letting her children cross the street by themselves. I've seen her so exhausted that she lay on top of the fence with her legs dangling on each side, just taking a nap.

But there is no doubt that there is a wild and dangerous side to them. Raccoons live in trees and engage in horrible fights with snapping and growling going on for hours at night. My friend Jerilynn, her husband Rusty, and their dog were camping out when raccoons raided their food supply, in their tent, and their dog tried to fight. Jerilynn dived into the fray to save her dog and got badly clawed. Later she was standing in line at a bank when she heard somebody in line ahead of her ask a friend, "Did you hear about that couple that got ate up by the raccoons up at the lake?"

We try to get along with our natural neighbors, but I draw the line at any creature who might come inside, like ants, rats, and mice; or who might carry rabies, like bats, foxes, skunks, and raccoons; or who might want to leave stinky piles of poop under my deck.

Our next step was to see what Google advised. Don't feed them, it said. We don't. We don't keep pets so don't have food sitting out. I have a compost pile for garden waste and vegetable matter from my kitchen, but raccoons don't seem to like moldy green peppers any more than I do.

Google advised trying repellent: Irish Spring soap, peppermint, and coyote urine. As it happened, I had two bars of Irish Spring soap in the bathroom cabinet, unused because my husband doesn't like its odor, either. We placed the soap near the raccoons' portal. We turned on the critter-cam. The raccoons sauntered past the soap like it wasn't even there.

Trying peppermint was convenient. My garden includes bunches of mint: peppermint, spearmint, sweet mint, rank wild mint, horehound mint, catnip mint and chocolate mint. I wondered if mint wasn't just an invitation to raccoons—it smells just like Girl Scout cookies. I pulled up an arm load of mint and placed it just where the raccoons crawled under the deck. The critter cam showed raccoons ignoring the mint.

I went to the hardware store. "Do you sell coyote urine?" I asked.

Well, of course they did. The clerk sent me to a shelf full of animal repellents for mice, rats, moles, rabbits, deer, and yes, raccoons. I read the label on the package of coyote urine. It was good for house cats, not for raccoons.

I chose a black pepper compound that was supposed to repel raccoons. We watched on the critter cam. The raccoons didn't even stop to sniff, let alone sneeze, at the black pepper barrier.

"We need the urine of a big, mean, aggressive animal," my husband stated. Did he mean a horse, maybe? Our neighbors' horses are pretty stinky, but I didn't want our deck smelling like a horse. Jerry just pointed to himself.

Now imagine a man of a certain age who sometimes has difficulty when he needs to go. He had the foresight to turn off the security cameras so he made no movie of his effort. He stood there a while. And a while. But then he succeeded.

We reviewed the security cameras the next day. The raccoons did not appear. After we checked to make sure nobody was hiding under the deck, we sealed it off with one-quarter-inch galvanized mesh. We think we have won this wildlife war.

CHAPTER 21

Rodentia

When we moved into this house in 2009, Jerry talked about getting some chickens, but I vetoed that idea. I've lived near chickens, and they stink. Besides, we'd agreed to having no house plants and no pets so that we would be free to travel whenever we wished. Although we've slipped a bit on that count, we did not acquire chickens. Instead, we started feeding wild birds. If we weren't home to serve them, we were confident they'd be fine on their own. The nearby shrub-steppes, orchards, yards, and un-developed lots would offer them a plenitude of seeds and insects to eat. We'd feed them more for our enjoyment than for their survival.

We set up critter cameras and found out right away that we were feeding more than birds. Where we'd scattered chicken scratch on the ground, the nighttime camera showed glittering eyes of field mice.

Field mice are a mere 3 to 4 inches long, plus tails about as long as their bodies. They are brownish gray with round ears and beady black eyes. Our house is well sealed, so we weren't concerned about their getting inside, and having a few in the yard didn't bother me. However, we kept seeing more and more, then rats joined the pack.

One evening when we saw a rat running on the top rail of our chain-link fence, we decided that we had to make changes. We stopped feeding birds except from hanging feeders, and except for tossing one scoop of chicken scratch on the ground in the morning. By the end of each day, a rotation of birds, including sparrows, finches, doves, and quail, has passed through the yard, and there was not a kernel of scratch left on the ground to entice mice or rats. Our problem disappeared into the fields. Like I heard a guy from a health department say, you can give a rodent a chaise longue and a leisure suit, but it won't stay if it has nothing to eat.

Whether it was mice or a rat, I'm not sure, but I suspect a packrat—during the winter, a rodent crawled under the heavy plastic cover on our barbeque and packed the grill area with grass. Unfortunately, a rat took a liking to the engine compartment of Jerry's pick-up. Some commentators on the internet said that rats are attracted to the insulation on electrical cords, and we couldn't have rats ruining a nice new truck. We put some natural "mouse mint" under the hood, and of course, the rat just laughed at that. We got some rat poison from the hardware store and used it to no effect—not surprisingly, because the fine print explained that the "poison" was not toxic. Finally, we got serious with a nerve toxin. It injured a massive rat that didn't die, but crawled into a bucket and twitched around and couldn't get out. We had to kill it with a bullet.

A friend turned his rat problem into art. A packrat gathered the poop the family's golden retriever had dumped in the yard and stacked it in a neat pile in the garden shed. After cleaning the shed, the poet wrote about it. He proves that a true artist can find inspiration anywhere. In part, his poem says:

> a little mountain, the kind of thing my daughters
>
> might have scooped together in the fall and left
>
> for the faeries if it weren't a perfectly conical accretion
>
> of turds....

{from "The Seconds," in *Not For Luck*, by Derek Sheffield, East Lansing, Wheelbarrow Books (2021)}

CHAPTER 22

Lagomorph, the Rabbit

I never see wild rabbits in the yard in person, but when snow coats the yard, I see their paw prints everywhere. When I saw prints around a hole beneath the tool shed, we set up a critter camera and captured the image of a tiny rabbit going in and out. We also caught sight of a domestic cat staring into the rabbit hole. The camera's poor resolution made the rabbit look like it was wearing spectacles.

I knew that pygmy rabbits were endemic to the shrub-steppe environment across the Columbia River from us, and I knew that they were endangered. The state was attempting to breed them in captivity and to release them back into the wild. In all probability, the tiny backyard rabbit we saw was a cotton tail, not a pygmy. Like Gil Grisson says on CSI: Vegas (Quoting Theodore Woodward, MD), "When you hear hoofbeats, think horses, not zebras." I wished it was a pygmy. I would welcome such a sign that the rabbit was making a comeback. Hope springs eternal.

CHAPTER 23

The Birds

Our region is one of the best bird-watching areas in the United States. Birds are drawn here by the wide diversity of habitat lying all within a perimeter of just a few miles: from the highest altitude down, we have snow-covered alpine areas, canopied evergreen forests of fir and spruce, hilly woodlands of Ponderosa pine, open prairies, the shrub-steppe, plus riverine and lacustrine wetlands. A major migratory flyway passes overhead.

When we moved here in 2009, my late father-in-law gave us a copy of *Sibley's Guide to Birds*, and I began to check off the species I'd see, taking credit for a sighting only if I were sure of the I.D. or an expert birder verified it for me. By now, I've listed about 200 species on my life list, and I have counted fifty of those that I have seen just within our subdivision. I'm a mere duffer. Friends from the local chapter of the Audubon Society name closer to 1,000 species on their life lists.

Not all fifty have come within our fence. I'll mention only those species we see from our house or inside the yard every day, depending on the season, since some are migratory. I'll begin with the skyscape.

Eagles

We see Golden Eagles the year 'round. They look all dark until they wheel into the sun, then the Golden earns its name. I wrote in my *Book of Birds:*

To a Golden Eagle

Your bird-book picture paints you the color of dirt

as nondescript as winter finches

before their breeding colors show

You aren't the only wide-winged sailor

soaring through our western scabland sky

Cranes and Ravens ride here, too.

The fact of your flight—like that of any bird

—amazes—but only you,

tipped toward sunshine, turn to burnished gold.

The Bald Eagle is here the year 'round, too. It is intent on flying its mission from the Columbia River to the hills in a no-nonsense straight line, white head and white rump gleaming in the sun.

Turkey Vultures

The biggest birds we see are the migratory Turkey Vultures, always in a flock, here only for the summer. No doubt there is a mathematical name for the pattern of their flight—they circle around a point, while the point moves down river in a straight line. Their flight describes a shape we made with stick pens and bottled ink in penmanship class in the fifth grade. Their flight looks the most effortless of all the birds. They just coast, barely fluttering their wingtips from time to time.

People react with repugnance to the mention of Turkey Vultures because they eat carrion, but from a distance, they are graceful. A South American novel that I read years ago mentions vultures perched on trees at the outskirts of villages. The mention was simply a landmark for approaching a village. It carried no association with death—the vultures were just a common species, like seagulls at the garbage dump, or crows at the Walmart parking lot.

Vultures locate the carrion they eat by odor. In years past, it was thought that other birds didn't have a sense of smell, then scientists found a structure in a bird's head that appeared to be an organ for detecting odors. I have to think that other birds can smell, if not as acutely as do vultures. When I hung a cylindrical birdfeeder only two feet off the ground amid the two foot tall peony bushes in our yard and filled it with nijer seed, American Goldfinches found it within minutes. They had to have smelled it; it wasn't visually conspicuous and they weren't daily visitors otherwise.

Osprey

The Osprey is migratory, too. I've wondered if it arrives and departs on an exact schedule like the legendary return of swallows to the Mission at San Juan Capistrano, on precisely March 19 every year. (I understand that when the Mission was remodeled, the swallows relocated to a nearby freeway underpass.) I noted our local Ospreys arriving on April Fool's Day in 2021, and in 2022, a week or so later than that, but I wasn't close enough to a nest to be confident of an exact arrival date. I'm equally unclear on the date they depart for Central America. One day they simply aren't there.

In the meantime, the Ospreys add to prior years' nests, enlarging them with sticks three or four feet long, and in one case, decorating it with a long yellow ribbon of crime scene tape. They are impressively successful at seeing fish and capturing them in the dark flowing water of the Columbia River. They are adept at flipping their catch in mid-air to hold it in an aerodynamic position as they fly it to their nests of clamoring chicks, but they are messier once they get it home. The ground beneath their nests is littered with small fish and fish parts.

The Ospreys are conspicuous, nesting on platforms that are the tallest structures on parcels close to the river. Without a platform, Ospreys will nest on the highest posts they can find, which unfortunately might clutter up a communication tower, a bridge truss, or a utility pole.

The last time I walked on a pedestrian bridge across the Columbia, I saw Ospreys peering at me from all the nooks and crannies in the bridge, glaring with eyes that were as mean-looking as the eyes of an NFL linebacker.

Great Blue Heron

Another very big bird traversing our air space is the Great Blue Heron, wending his way between the Columbia River and the irrigation reservoir, Lake Cortez, in the middle of our neighborhood. We see the heron flying with its long legs extending far behind it like a rudder, and comment, "There goes the old man." We have no idea whether the heron we see is male or female, young or old. However, when it stands on an embankment near the water, its long neck tucked into a U, it looks like an old man wrapped in a gray blanket, his shoulders hunched against the cold. I wrote:

Great Blue Heron

Ubiquitous.

The great blue heron is so well known

that everyone calls him "G-B-H,"

 like "JFK" or "FDR",

so presidential

he is named by initials alone.

My *Sibley's* bird book says that generally, the Great Blue Heron is a solitary bird, a night-time fisherman. That surprises me. I see it frequently in the daytime, and I know of a tree three miles away that is a heron rookery. Thirteen huge stick GBH nests turn the tree into a heron condominium.

Canada Geese

They are "Canada Geese," not "Canadian Geese," okay? Their name is their type, not their citizenship. Thousands and thousands of them populate our autumn air space. They look identical, like wave upon wave of uniformed clones.

And they honk. Years ago when my office mates and I were chatting around the water cooler, somebody wondered aloud why geese honked in flight. I told them what my father had told me: He said that they lower a membrane over their eyes to protect their eyes during flight. They honk to help place themselves in their V formations for long flights so that they don't have to see precisely where they are going. My colleagues laughed. It never occurred to me that Dad might not have been accurate—he was a keen observer of nature—but admittedly, he was a plumber, not an ornithologist.

Ravens and Crows

Like the Bald Eagle, the Ravens and American Crow seem intent on going about their business, flying in straight lines between the Columbia and the foothills. They are all work and no play—that is, until the wind comes blowing hard down the river, then they like to play. They fly close to the ground, then rise up into the wind and flip completely over, like hot-dog pilots at an air show.

I've been told that Ravens stay in the hills, but I've seen them down here below the hills and close to the river. I'm certain of the identification of the players I've seen. Crows have squared-off tails; Ravens' tails are wedge-shaped.

I was hiking in the deep forest when I heard dulcet tones like an opera contralto warming up her voice—I froze, and listened, trying to figure out what sort of musician I was hearing—then, singing lessons were over, and I heard the familiar "Caw caw caw" of a crow.

Twice I have seen crow funerals. A neighbor shot a crow out of his cherry tree and left its body on his lawn. Crows flew in from all over the area to scream their displeasure. The second time, a crow was struck by a car and lay dead on the roadway median. Again, dozens of crows flew to the site and screamed and screamed.

Many times we have seen the eagle flying past our house, being chased by a crow, which was being chased by House Sparrows. The sparrows fly at the crow from high and behind like jet fighters in a dogfight, until eventually the eagle and the crow are driven away.

Red-Tailed Hawk, Kestrel, and Sharp-Shinned Hawks

The Red-tailed Hawk perches on the cross-arms of a utility pole in the orchard across the street and downhill from us. It has flown close enough to buzz our house on its hunting missions but has not attacked the smaller birds in our yard. The Red-tail that we see regularly is light-colored, a yellow "morph."

The little American Kestrel caught our attention by hovering for a considerable time high above our neighboring orchard, then diving at its prey. It's a colorful bird with a black-and-orange striped back, blue-gray sides, and yellow breast with black speckles.

The Kestrel is our smallest falcon. It flies so fast that it can capture other birds mid-air, so it's also called a "Sparrow Hawk." It hauls its victims to the top of a neighbor's spruce tree and eviscerates them there. Like the other falcons around here, including the Merlin, Prairie Falcon and Peregrine Falcon, it is marked with a black teardrop under its eye, like the tattoos on confessed murderers in the movies. It's so aggressive that its murderous tattoo is appropriate.

The Sharp-shinned Hawk matches the Kestrel for its aggression against smaller birds. The "Sharpie" is small, as hawks go, only about 11 inches long. It has a hooked beak, a dark gray back, an orange belly, and a long tail crossed with dark stripes. It is a frequent visitor to our yard, perching on the top rail of the chain-link fence, preying. It surveys the area around the bird feeders for any unwary sparrow, finch, or California Quail, then attacks. I've seen it press a quail to the ground and kill it, even though the quail is nearly as big as it is. The Sharpie will chase and follow other birds right into the shrubbery where they try to hide. Once I saw the Sharpie follow sparrows under the dense rose shrubbery in the corner of my yard until it came to the fence, then it couldn't figure out how to get out. I had to approach it from outside the fence and prod it with a broomstick to get it to turn around to make its escape.

Two Kinds of Blackbirds

The spring brings in a migration of Red-winged Blackbirds with their noisy call, three notes rising in pitch, "Coke-a-Ree!" I heard a child call it, "The bird with a sunset on its wing," and indeed, it has an arced patch of red outlined by an arc of yellow, albeit upside down for a sunset. Redwings visit the feeder, but soon wander off to nest in a cattail marsh. (Yes, we live in a desert, as measured by precipitation. However, the nearby Cascades get plenty of snow. When it melts, it seeps through layers of sandstone, through vesicles in basalt, through canyons and run-out zones, and it does hydrate marshes.)

Brewer's Blackbird is about the size of a Red-winged Blackbird. It is glossy black except for a white ring around each eye. It flies in a tight circle spiraling down into the yard. Usually, several arrive at the same time, and one will perch on the prow of our roof to stand guard. If I walk into the yard, it warns its cohorts that I am an intruder. It makes a gurgling noise that sounds exactly like a toilet flushing. It has many other vocalizations too, including a melodious song.

The Brewer's Blackbird nests in trees. In our neighborhood, they nest in the ponderosa pines and black cottonwood trees in the park in the middle of our subdivision, just a block from my yard. When they have chicks, they don't want me to be close. Several at a time will fly at my head, screaming, and will follow me even when I try to walk away.

The American Robin

The American Robin arrives in the springtime. It's fearless around humans, but not aggressive. However, it will attack its own reflection in a window, a sliding glass door, or a car mirror, and never seems to give up. It is equally persistent about building a nest.

When one began building on top of our outdoor security light, Jerry removed its materials several times over, out of concern that the hot halogen bulb could ignite the bird's mess of dried grass and other debris. Every time he removed it, the robin reconstructed it, until Jerry piled non-flammable material on top of the light to crowd the bird out. Jerry had to act quickly because he has a tremor when he tries to stand. He grabbed whatever he found first to deter the robin. That's where, eventually, I found the can of stewed tomatoes that had gone missing from my pantry.

No bird loves the birdbath so much as the robin. Every day, any time of day, a robin splashes vigorously. I think of a 1950s-era song, "Splish-splash, I was takin' a bath/ 'long about Saturday night..." Then the robin perches on our garden bench to let the wind blow-dry its rumpled feathers.

Doves

The Eurasian Collared Doves rotate into the yard mid-morning. Appropriately, they are dove gray, with a line ending in points across the backs of their necks — their own logo, as distinctive as a Nike's "Swoosh" or Coca-Cola's "Dynamic Ribbon Device." They join the House Sparrows on the ground, sampling the chicken scratch, then they fly off, sounding their raucous screech. They are not native. One theory is that that they were introduced into North America by bridal couples releasing doves at their weddings. However, most are gray and only a few are the white Turtle Doves we associate with weddings.

Because Eurasian Collared Doves have become so widespread, birders are concerned that they will crowd out the smaller, native Mourning Dove. The Mourning Doves aren't as visible as the Collared Doves in my yard, but I hear them constantly, "Hoo-huh-hoo, hoo," much like a Great Horned Owl, but without the Owl's deeper-pitched voice. Alfred, Lord Tennyson wrote of "the cooing of innumerable doves." On summer days around here, the more appropriate phrase would be "the incessant cooing of doves."

House Sparrows and White-crowned Sparrows

The most numerous of any bird species that visits our yard is the House Sparrow (English Sparrow). It is here every day of the year. I recognize the male by his cap that is so gray it makes him look old. They are social, staying in flocks, chattering. They nest in our neighbor's dense cedar hedge, and I see them diving headlong into the greenery as though they could see where they were going. They feed in a flock on the ground for a few seconds, but they are peripatetic, flying, returning, repeating. That must discourage predators—they never sit still long enough to be caught.

House Sparrows are so plentiful that even a bird-loving conservationist I know has wished them all dead, cursing them for outcompeting native species.

The House Sparrows feed on the ground, but they are so ravenous that we keep them out of the cylindrical hanging feeder so that other birds can eat. House Sparrows will not perch on the feeder if anything is hanging over their heads. We twisted a piece of wire into a halo a few inches greater in diameter than the feeder and attached a bail handle. We suspended it over the top of the feeder, then attached some garden ties to hang down from it. (I've thought of replacing the garden tie danglers with a string of pretty beads.) Avoiding the halo of dangling things, the Sparrows have not perched on the feeder since.

The White-crowned Sparrows, named obviously for the white stripes on their heads, are not so common and not so social as their cousins, the House Sparrows. They are also fearless about perching on the hanging feeder, so they get to eat the good stuff.

House Finches and American Goldfinches

House Finches and American Goldfinches occupy our yard for the entire year. They bring a seasonal change of color to the yard that is as dramatic as spring itself. The drab little House Finch puts on a bold red face, breast, and rump. I wrote a take on that in my *Book of Birds*:

Thoughts Turn

Spring   brings

raging hormones

to the wild House Finch.

His face feathers redden

no sweet tweeter, he--

this is lust

not blushing.

Similarly, the male American Goldfinch turns from brown to bright yellow with black at its eyes and black and white on its wings. When it can choose among feeders, it has a strong preference for nijer seed.

When the Goldfinch flies cross-country instead of just flitting around in the yard, its flight describes a perfect sine curve, going up and coming down in a curve with perfect symmetry, up at 45 degrees, down at 45 degrees. That maximizes its range per wingbeat. Once that was the goal of soldiers firing cannons: if an angle is too steep, the cannoneer has to be too close to his target to be safe because the cannonball doesn't go forward far enough before falling to the ground. If the initial angle is too low, the flight is so low that gravity causes it to intersect the ground before it uses up its kinetic energy. The Goldfinch is an efficient little cannonball.

California Quail

We began feeding birds in the yard to try to attract California Quail. We had just moved to North Central Washington from the cool, damp, west side of the Cascades which does not have quail. We enjoyed being able to leave the patio door open to let a breeze blow through the house on warm June days. That day we were playing rock music, a bit loudly. While we played some Van Halen we heard an odd note playing at perfectly regular intervals in the music. It was a California Quail interjecting its appreciation. "Van Halen," it said, "Van Halen."

Besides calling to the rhythm of "Van Halen," the California Quail have many other vocalizations. Sometimes they sound a single note, then pause, then sound again, over and over again. That voice sounds like a man trying to sound like a woman, "Awk! (pause) Awk!" Other times, they herd their chicks through the yard with a soft "cluck cluck cluck."

California Quail troop through the yard all year 'round. They form flocks, sometimes as few as six, sometimes more than twenty. They walk past in lines, their topknots bobbing, preferring not to fly if they don't have to. "Goofy," my friend Susan calls them, and the moniker fits.

If the flock of quail is feeding on the ground and they are alarmed by a predator, they instantly spread out in a circle as perfect as the ripples a rock makes when it's dropped in a pond, then they freeze. They look like stones. They look like they should have cartoon bubbles over their heads that say, "You can't see me! You can't see me."

The Quail have two prominent survival adaptations. First, their spreading out and freezing might sacrifice one of their number for the sake of the flock, but a predator can chase them in only one direction at a time, and the others get away. Second, their clutches are enormous, increasing the likelihood that some will survive infant mortality. When one pair nested in a dimple in the ground behind my compost pile, the female deposited thirteen eggs in a single clutch.

Even gentle Quail can be aggressive in a flock. On one autumn day, they came flowing out of the yard, out of the swath of sagebrush and rabbit brush across the street from us, out of lots up the street, and I counted some 200 of them walking down the street. A neighbor's cat approached them to investigate, and the birds turned on him. They chased the cat until he ran and hid under a parked pickup truck.

I once saw an antique basket woven by an Native American of Northern California. It was decorated with quail topknots all the way around its rim. To an omnivore, quail are squabs, which are edible. I understand that people must eat. Perhaps it was a gesture of appreciation for the quail, to have its finest feathers displayed that way, but it made me sad.

Red-shafted Northern Flicker

The Northern Red-shafted Flicker who visits the yard serves as the neighborhood rock band. He wears a showy costume, a cape of feathers on his back that is tan with black stripes and red on the underside, a black amulet on its buff spotted breast, a streak of red under its eye, and a red spot on the back of his head. He calls from the yard with a long, strung-out call like the one that opens the Surfari's song "Wipe-Out," or it alights on a utility pole across the street and it drums. Sometimes it is just tapping for insects to eat, but other times, it pounds hard to make its presence known. Sometimes it finds a metal pole to pound on and becomes a real head-banging rocker.

At the Wenatchee River Salmon Festival one autumn I helped out at an educational birding booth. The North Central Washington Audubon Society taught a bit about birdwatching, handed out literature, and answered questions. The question we heard most frequently was "What do I do about Flickers pounding on my house?" There wasn't much we could advise, just, "Check your siding for insects, and wait it out. Their breeding season won't last forever."

Black-capped Chickadee

I hear the distinctive call of the Black-capped Chickadee much more frequently than I see the bird. His mating call has the rhythm of a pick-up line in a bar, "Poor me. Poor me." He also announces his name, "Chickadee-dee-dee." At the end of summer when the seeds of wild sunflowers are ripe, the Chickadees no longer cares who sees them. They come out of hiding to perch on the seed-heads of the flowers and works until every last seed is plucked out. Luckily, they are messy eatesr. They drops enough for the sunflowers to reseed themselves, assuring next year's crop.

Swallows

The swallows are summer residents. We see the Tree Swallows, with their blue-green backs and white undersides flying high overhead, darting in erratic paths after flying insects.

An old barn stands at the edge of a neighbor's orchard. It has an excavated basement with a wide door for a tractor, standing open permanently. The Barn Swallows, with orange bellies, move in every spring, then disappear abruptly every autumn. During the summer, when I walk past, they deploy like jet fighters, scrambling to intercept invaders in the Capitol's air space. They swoop at me and follow me until they deem the threat of me has abated.

As with Ospreys, I am tempted to note the spring arrival and autumn departure dates of the swallow to see if they are precise to the day, but I've never been quite attentive enough to notice until suddenly, they are here, or suddenly, they are gone.

Hummingbirds

Caliope, Black-chinned, Anna's and Rufous Hummingbirds appear around here. I've seen the Anna's and the Rufous in my yard. Anna's have been documented to spend winters here, even though the maps in my bird books would have them confined to more temperate areas on the western, far side of the Cascades. True to their reputations, the hummingbirds are drawn to red flowers. In my yard, red gladiolas bloom in the front yard every year, but they don't bloom until midsummer. From time to time, I've seen an Anna's nose into a pink rose flower and a Rufous probing the tubular pink flowers of monarda (bee balm). But time and time again, on the very day the gladiola blooms, the Hummingbirds will be here to greet it. It stays for the bright blooms of the zinnia.

Great Horned Owl

Deep. Sonorous. With the tone quality of a human voice, the Great Horned Owl hoots, "Hoo, Huh Hoo Hoo." When one hoots, another replies in a slightly different pitch. Their call and response can go on for an hour during the autumn nights of their breeding season. They sound like they are right outside the house, but we have spotted them only a few times. Once, Jerry was sitting in the darkened living room looking up at the night sky. He thought he saw a large bird fly up to the peak of our roof. He called me, and we took a flashlight outside to our deck. We switched on the light and aimed it at the roof for only a second, not wanting to scare the bird. It was a Great Horned. It simply looked down on us and didn't stay.

My dramatic encounter with a Great Horned Owl occurred in July in the middle of the day. I had walked about three blocks from my house to the edge of Lake Cortez, the irrigation reservoir in the middle of our neighborhood. One lot on the lake belongs to our home-owner's association and is not developed except for occasional mowing to allow access to the lake. With some dense understory and tall cottonwoods, it's an excellent bird-watching place. There, on a low limb of a small maple, sat a Great Horned Owl, looking at me from no more than 20 feet away. It was so immobile that I thought it was somebody's robotic toy. I looked around toward neighboring houses to see who might be punking me, leading me into taking photographs of a dummy. I didn't see anybody. Then the owl lifted one feathered leg and stretched its vicious-looking talons toward me. No toy robot would be programmed to do that! I quickly and quietly left the owl alone.

Some people think an owl is a bad omen, but my mother always taught that it was lucky to have an owl in the household (outdoors only, of course.)

Steller's Jay

I think that the Steller's Jay is one of the prettiest birds in our yard. Its head and crest are black, and the rest of its body is deep, scintillating blue. It is an expert mimic. Besides its unique raucous cry, it is well known for replicating the call of the Red-tailed Hawk, and I have heard it do a convincing cat. What's mysterious is why it would want to.

I suspect that the Steller's Jay mimics to warn its community that a threat is present, and it might be mentioning precisely which threat it is. I've seen and heard it mimic the Red-Tailed Hawk when the hawk was present. That roused the sparrows that attacked the hawk, sparing the jay from having to do the fighting himself.

Steller's Jays are pair-bonded. Often they fly into the feeder together. When one slammed into our window and fell to the ground unmoving, I thought it was dead. Its mate flew down and stood next to it for at least ten minutes. Maybe it sensed life, because then, amazingly, the bird roused itself and flew off. The loyalty of the mate, where cats could have gotten them both, was touching.

Towhees and Juncos

Winter Brings the Towhees and Juncos. My father called Spotted Towhees "Rain Robins," because the winter weather brought them to the yard, and they do resemble Robins. They have the size and shape of a Robin, its black head and red along the breast, but the Towhee also has a white belly, white spots on its dark wings, and very red eyes. Its beak is short and stout for crunching, not longer and thinner like a Robin's worm-puller. The Towhee is notable for its vigorous scratching away the leaf litter under the garden plants, going after whatever it finds to eat.

Winter also brings the Juncos down from the foothills into the yard. A Junco was the first bird I learned to identify from a book. It's a small bird that is black on the head, beak, and eyes, gray-brown on its back, and light on its breast. Properly, it's a "Dark-eyed Junco," but it's an "Oregon Junco" in the color combination it wears around here. Its color varies elsewhere in the nation.

The Covid-19 pandemic shut-downs kept me home and away from birding field trips, but along came "Merlin" just in time to help me out. It's a free cellphone app from the Cornell University Ornithology Lab. It listens to a bird call, records it, identifies the bird, and offers information about that species. This spring when the local birds were giddy with their breeding season, I stood at the edge of Lake Cortez and launched Merlin. Within five minutes and six seconds, it identified seventeen bird calls. It didn't count the Great Blue Heron and the Bald Eagle that passed through my birding site at the time, because they were both silent. Of the seventeen calls it picked up, all were common, which makes my point. My small homestead is a veritable Wild Kingdom of birds.

REFERENCES

Gessner, David: *Soaring With Fidel: An Osprey Odyssey From Cape Cod to Cuba and Beyond* Boston, Beacon Press (2008).

Sibley, David Allen: *The Sibley Guide to Birds*, New York, Alfred A. Knopf (2000)

Sampson, Susan: *Book of Birds*, Wild Leek Press, Emory University, Atlanta, GA (2018)

CHAPTER 24

Cats

Domestic cats, like pet dogs, inevitably are a part of our subdivision environment. Our chain-link fence keeps the dogs out, but there is no excluding a feline. Birders vilify them for predation on songbirds, but in our neighborhood they have yet to be ambitious or quick enough to catch any.

Maybe Jerry hoped chumming them with cat food would keep them away from birds. Whatever his theory, he has befriended a couple of them. One is a bashful long-haired gray-and-white cat that waits quietly at the edge of the deck in the morning for food to appear. He never makes a sound, never comes close enough to touch. He has had his travails — we've seen wounds on his head and flanks that he licked bald until he recovered.

The black-and-white cat who appeared in our neighborhood one day was plainly domesticated. He sauntered into the house, climbed up on Jerry's lap, napped on the sofa — but he never stayed. He strongly preferred to be outdoors most of the time. At least three neighbors asked, "Does anybody know whose cat this is? He's been coming to our house every day to eat, but he never stays."

A responsible young pet-owning neighbor took the black-and-white to the Humane Society to get him neutered. The vet informed him that the cat had already been fixed. Young people today aren't farm kids; they don't know how to examine a tomcat's genitals to check. Instead of having surgery, the cat was fitted with a chip, so that if somebody took him to animal control, the neighbor would be notified and return the cat to its four houses. Like the pet meme says, "Dogs have masters. Cats have staff."

Part IV

Plants

CHAPTER 25

Stylin' in the Garden

Gardens have their styles. Think of photos of gardens in the center of Paris — square flower beds edged with rows of identical bedding plants amid paved walkways, giving a sense of formality to them. Think of English cottage gardens with their herbaceous (perennial) borders, crowded with flowering plants. Think of Japanese gardens with green backdrops around temples or ponds, moss-covered stones, shrubs pruned to expose the curves of their trunk, perhaps raked sand, all conveying a sense of tranquility. Think of an American suburban yard with a smooth lawn bordered with a few neat flowering shrubs set in mulched flower beds. Think of Sun City, Arizona, yards covered with rock except for a palm tree and a few large cacti. Think of a restauranteur's small kitchen garden with neat rows of herbs, onions, and pretty red-veined leaves of Swiss Chard, posed to entice customers inside.

Garden designers advise dividing gardens into rooms, each with lines leading into a view. An older gardener warns to keep the garden feasible to maintain—we won't always be spry enough to juggle 40-pound bags of fertilizer, she reminds us, and install handrails.

When we were new to the desert, I asked for gardening advice from another couple who had also relocated from the wet side of the mountains. "You can grow anything," they said. "Just don't plant shrubs under the eaves because snow falling off the roof will crush them."

I wish my small yard could express all of the popular styles, but for starters, another design principle pertains: form follows function. The shape of my yard is determined first, by the size of my standard subdivision lot, one tenth of an acre or 4,356 square feet. Some people have houses with larger footprints than that. My lot is fan-shaped, being a corner lot with curved frontage from the west side around to the north side. The house with attached garage occupies about 1,800 feet. There is a concrete patio 10 feet wide and the length of the house on the south side. Decks wrap around the house on parts of the south and west sides. A paved driveway the width of the double-wide garage covers part of the north side. The curved lot-line running from southwest to northeast follows an embankment that is approximately 10 feet tall and maybe 8 feet deep; too steep to stand on without something to hang on to, and not suitable for gardening.

Further, although it's irrigated, we live in a desert where lawns aren't practical, so except for a small former dog run in the backyard (east side), the grass is gone, replaced by gray cobblestones near the foundation, reddish landscaping shale through the front (west) side, and a pea-gravel walking path along the south. What's left, the perimeter, is available to be gardened.

What remains uncovered is densely planted, varied and lush, and being most like the English style, it demands constant maintenance.

I wish I could find the exact comment by the late poet W.S. Merwin that I read once — he distinguished landscaping from a garden, and a garden from a wilderness or a forest. He said that humans could never recreate a forest, but he did what he could by creating a garden filled with as many species of palm trees as he could collect from all over the world. He said that the difference between landscaping and a garden is that a garden is never finished. My yard cannot compare to his plantation. However, I think he would agree that my over-planted and somewhat spontaneously chaotic yard qualifies as a garden.

REFERENCES

Abell, Sam: *Seeing Gardens,* The National Geographic Society, Washington, D.C. (2000)

Conran, Terence and Pearson, Dan: *The Essential Garden Book, Getting Back to Basics,* New York, Crown Publishers (1998)

Roach, Margaret: *A Way to Garden, a Hands-on Primer for Every Season,* New York, Clarkson N. Potter (1998)

CHAPTER 26

Shall I Steal a Start?

Gardening is a part of my family's culture. On the south side of Chicago during the Great Depression of the 1930s, my maternal grandmother traded loaves of home-made bread for droppings from a peddler's horse to keep her backyard garden fertilized. My paternal grandfather grew loganberries, strawberries, and red potatoes. My paternal grandmother grew flowers, including bright nasturtiums in a flower box and trilliums transplanted from the forest into a shady corner next to the porch. The trilliums grew to two feet tall over the years and were never to be picked, since picking the flower would kill the plant. My mother and father always kept a "Victory Garden" for vegetables to help feed the family in case of shortages. Mom would grow begonias and flowers as well, but dad said he wouldn't grow anything he couldn't eat, so he focused on the loganberries, rhubarb, scallions, cabbages, parsnips, carrots, beans, peas, and to my disgust, rutabagas.

My garden reflects the values of my family elders. They

shared plants, lore, and taunts the way they'd share reci-
pes. If you steal a start, it's sure to grow. The best fertilizer is poultry manure, applied early in the spring. When a
plant thrived, "What did you do, pee on it?" (A neighbor
in Snoqualmie, WA, confessed that she'd tried that one
night, for her rhododendron.)

My friends and I carry on the tradition of exchanging
plants. I pass on starts from my loganberry patch that have
"layered": the tips of vines resting on the ground have sent
down roots, creating a new plant that I cut loose and give
away. My garden is richer for my friends' donations, including Egyptian walking onions, golden raspberries, lilies
of the valley, yucca, and horseradish. It's such an esoteric
array that it would never fit in a neatly landscaped yard.

CHAPTER 27

The Edibles

Part of my yard serves as my kitchen garden, supposedly keeping me stocked with fresh vegetables. I have to admit that my efforts have been more of a daydream than a reward.

I have wanted a kitchen garden since seeing one outside one of those upscale wineries with a fine restaurant and a chic gift shop that I visited near Casa Grande, Arizona. The tidy rows of bright fluffy lettuces, dark spinach, red or yellow stems of Swiss chard, and the hollow, pointed stems of onions gave me a sense of cozy hominess.

I wanted my kitchen garden to have strawberries. I have wanted to grow strawberries since I was ten years old. That summer, a farmer near Siletz, Oregon, on the coast, planned to plow under his field and replace his crop with a newer variety. At the time, strawberries had hulls that were somewhat sunken into the flesh on the top of the berry. Newer varieties held their hulls away from the fruit, almost on a neck, and were easier to clean. Their hulls could be sliced off rather than having to be dug out. The farmer opened his field to the public to pick his last crop themselves, and my family quickly filled enough flats to make fresh strawberry shortcake and to cook down into jam. Never again have I enjoyed such an abundance of strawberries.

Big, beautiful strawberries appear in the grocery stores, but to me, too often they have very little flavor, like those big, shiny, Red Delicious apples that stocked the markets in years past.

My efforts to grow strawberries have failed repeatedly. My plants grew lush green leaves, and tried to spread by runners, but they didn't bloom and set berries. I consulted with high school classmates who'd grown up on farms, and following their instructions, I cultivated, fertilized, and watered, to no avail. I tried growing them in a strawberry barrel that I placed on a saucer with wheels so I could rotate it into the sun. The effort wasn't worth it.

Finally, I germinated a package of seeds for tiny Alpine-type strawberries. I got the seeds mail order from Thomas Jefferson's Monticello. Quickly, they filled the raised bed I'd put them in, spilled runners onto adjacent walkways, bloomed, and fruited, setting bright red fruits no larger than a split pea. They're nice. They're sweet, although they don't taste like the larger species. It must take an acre of them to produce enough fruit to make a shortcake. The birds in the yard are welcome to those I've tired of picking.

I'm not the only would-be grower who has failed at berries around here. A commercial orchardist set blueberry plants out in one of his fields. I figured that if he could grow blueberries, I could, too. My plants sat in the ground as inert as garden gnomes, then they died. "Didn't you know?" a neighbor asked me. "He pulled his out, too."

I planted rows of pretty green vegetables for a kitchen garden.

"I don't eat green shit," my husband announced. He'd rather get his vitamins from a pharmacy. To some degree, I understand. During his early teenaged years, his father took a job with the U.S. State Department in Rio de Janeiro, Brazil. The Department indoctrinated the whole family before they left, teaching table manners (fork in the left hand, turned over into the mouth), and warned them to eat only cooked food, to drink only purified water. He followed the instructions like they were the Gospel, the Boy Scout laws, and the Criminal Code rolled into one. He was the only member of the family of four kids who didn't come home with worms in the gastrointestinal tract.

I needn't have worried about growing too much produce to eat by myself. The spinach, beets, and chard got leaf miners. The larva of the leaf miner insect is so tiny that it can invade the layer of green tissue between the upper and lower layer of cells of a thin leaf, leaving the leaves with grayish translucent windows.

By contrast, my rhubarb thrived. I fed it a generous dose of poultry manure early in the year, and acting on old family lore, I broke off any flowers, so all its energy went into growing stems. It was more than I could use, so keeping my pandemic distancing, I anonymously porch-bombed the home of a woman in her nineties whose rhubarb plant died out some years ago. She suspected the culprit right away and emailed me a thank you note before I even got home.

My one rhubarb plant produces enough stems that I could make rhubarb wine. I had an older friend who grew up on a farm in North Dakota who made rhubarb wine in gallon glass jugs. You let it work until you see the white crust form in the bottles; that's cream of tartar, he explained. His tasted pretty good, but when I think of fruit wine, I remember those teenage experiments with commercial grape juice in a jug, baker's yeast, and a balloon pulled over the neck of the bottle to signal when the fermentation was done. Godawful.

I live in onion country. The Walla Walla Sweet is local and in season, plentiful. I don't need to grow any. I do grow a handful of Egyptian walking onions because my cousin Jon gave me some. They send up hollow two-foot-tall stems that produce bulblets on top. The bulblets are so heavy that they tip the stems over. The bulblets, now on the ground, send down roots, grow new stems with bulblets to tip over, and that way, keep on walking.

I once had a neighbor, Mr. Diego, who was a ship's cook. Whenever he was home from the sea, he filled the neighborhood with the aroma of cooking onions. Working in my garden one morning, I smelled onions and thought of him, then realized I was smelling just the aroma of walking onions rubbing on my pantlegs.

The pride and joy of the edibles in my garden is my loganberry patch. Loganberries are a hybrid of blackberries and raspberries, as are marionberries and tayberries. My loganberries came from starts in my grandfather's garden, which he was cultivating at least as far back as the 1930s. My father grew some clones and gave some to me. They make big, rangy vines covered with prickles, so they aren't a logical choice for a small yard. However, I won't argue with success. By the 4th of July, their two-year-old vines set plump purple berries an inch or more long, oozing with delicious juice, and the plants are well on their way to growing the vines that will produce the next year's fruit. Two of my cousins grow the vines, too, as our way of keeping a tradition alive in our family. Marcia makes pie with her berries. Sam eats his straight. I make jelly that I can in jars to send to my family for Christmas. Any leftover juice ends up as cornstarch pudding.

Besides rhubarb and loganberries, the garden is great for herbs. Chives put out fresh stems and pretty purple flowers early in the spring. Oregano fills as much space as I give it and attracts a cloud of mason bees and hover flies. Italian flat-leafed parsley thrives, blooms, sets flowers, and self-seeds to assure next year's crop. The seeds germinate wherever they land–namely, everywhere. Garden sage will season the dressing to go with my Thanksgiving turkey (or Cornish game hen, depending on whether we can socialize by then.) There's French tarragon, which grows only from root cuttings. Italian basil and Thai basil from seed thrive among the tomato plants. There are mints: Crinkly-leafed dark green spearmint and peppermint and chocolate mint that I rooted from a sprig that a neighbor gave me; and pale, fuzzy-leafed horehound mint and catnip mint, lemon balm (melissa) and bee balm (monarda.) Sometimes a rank wild mint sneaks in among them, too. Mints are easy to identify—their stems are perfectly square, like the square-braided key fobs we used to make at Girl Scout camp. Fortunately, they are easy to grow. Unfortunately, they invade. Their shallow roots are easy to pull out, but the roots are brittle and any that breaks off sends up new shoots.

Chamomile came into my yard as a hitchhiker in a pot of something else from a plant nursery. I put it in a prime location in the yard, with sunlight, water, and rich soil. It promptly moved out. It reappeared in a dry pea-gravel walkway, succeeding just fine in the thin loess that the wind brings to the path. It threads its roots through the pores in the ground cloth beneath the gravel and sends down a tap root. Chamomile is a pretty little plant, six inches high with leaves so finely dissected that they look fuzzy, and a daisy-shaped flower with twelve white petals and a yellow center no larger than a ½ inch across.

Beatrice Potter told us that Peter Rabbit barely escaped being trapped in Mr. MacGregor's garden. He hid in a watering can, but caught cold there, so when he got home, his mother dosed him with chamomile tea. It's an ages-old folk remedy, but I'm sure that Mrs. Rabbit was using aversion therapy. It's a pretty flower, but it's rank! Its crushed leaves or flowers smell so nasty that any little rabbit forced to drink its tea as a cure for misbehavior would never stray again.

Chamomile has a cousin, wild pineapple weed, that looks the same as chamomile and grows in the dry, compact gravel of the roadway shoulder. Unlike its cousin, it has the pleasant smell of pineapple. I've never known it to be collected for a garden. These two cousins make a point: a plant is going to grow where it wants to grow, not where you want it to grow if the environment isn't just right.

Practically, the herbs produce more than I can hope to use, ever. At season's end, they go into the compost pile. When I turn over the compost, I smell them again. I have highly aromatic compost.

CHAPTER 28

The Exotics

Dad wouldn't grow what he couldn't eat, but Mom had more exotic tastes. Botanically, "exotic" just means originating in a distant, foreign place. It doesn't mean strikingly, excitingly, mysteriously different, like an "exotic dancer" doing a strip-tease behind feathers or fans, but to my mind, to a degree, the two definitions overlap.

The exotic plants imported to my yard include lavender lilacs, red lilies, pink peonies, red tulips, yellow daffodils, red-orange gladiolas, snapdragons and cosmos in crazy-quilt colors, zinnias red and orange enough to attract hummingbirds, and hollyhocks in white, yellow, and shades of red ranging from deep maroon to pale pink. Their brightness stands in high contrast to the gray-green and brown of our desert setting. They look like the dancer's fans and feathers!

I have pinks, those carnation ancestors noted for their spicy clove scent. I have fragrant violets that want to move right in and make themselves at home all over the yard, even in that thin layer of blown-in dirt lying between the ground cloth and the topping of landscaping rock. The problem is that I have to flatten myself on the ground to get my nose close enough to smell them.

I have calla lilies, orange and yellow. They are new to me, and I don't know how they will fare yet. I think that Diego Rivera admired them, given their presence in his paintings of Mexican women selling them by the armloads. I have always loved the smooth, simple lines of old-fashioned white callas. My mother hated them, because to her, they were funerary flowers.

I have a rose geranium growing in a big pot that will winter over in my heated garage. I found it at a nursery, mislabeled as "citronella," like those evil-smelling candles that are supposed to ward off mosquitoes at backyard barbeque parties. It's wonderful to brush its leaves, releasing the fragrance of roses.

I once met an artist whose paintings were limited to the muted, misty colors of the Pacific Northwest coast. She made a trip to Mexico and came back with her "mind blown." She began to add color to her works. I've been a tourist in Mexico, and I've seen miles of land as plain and brown as the hills of home, but reveled in colors within the churches, shops, gardens, restaurants, and other enclaves within the towns. "Mexicans have a great sense of humor," my husband commented, when he alighted in the brightly painted lobby of a Mexican airport or when he saw the bright yellow walls of the Mexican market near our neighborhood. It's the same with flower gardens. They brighten us.

CHAPTER 29

The Roses

The rose bushes in my front yard crowd together shoulder to shoulder, lining the entire inside of the fence. They are more than just a planting—they are a hobby. Even in my small yard I have historical plants and wild species. I know their names and their personalities like some people know their pets.

When I was still a teenager, my mother taught me a trick for growing roses. Our family was visiting the site of an abandoned hot springs spa. Its cabins had fallen and limber vines of a butterscotch yellow rose trailed over their remains. Mom told me to find a flower on a pencil-thick twig, and to break it off with a heel where the twig met the next larger branch. We kept it damp in a tissue until we got it home, then planted it in damp soil. It took root!

A decade or so later, in the 1970s, *Sunset, the Magazine of Western Living* ran an article about types of roses, like tall, stiff-branched climbers, bushy *rugosa* shrubs, and elegant modern hybrid teas with solitary blossoms on the top of tall stems. The hybrid tea type was ubiquitous and almost no other kind of rose was offered in plant nurseries at the time. I was living in Seattle in an old neighborhood with alleys dividing the blocks. Inspired by the article, I began watching for other types of roses reaching into alleys or growing in abandoned lots. I used Mom's trick, snitched cuttings from untended, overgrown plants, and rooted them.

Besides tucking the cuttings in pots to root, I pulled a plastic bag over the pots to create miniature greenhouses. I'd see the leaves fall off my collected twig, but then new growth would emerge from the leaf axils. Usually within about one month, I'd see new roots emerging from the bottom of the flowerpot, and I'd know that a new rose bush was ready to go into the ground.

Now, in the desert, starting a rose is trickier because summer days are too hot to use plastic for greenhouses, and without a cover, the plant can quickly dry out. However, over the last fifty years, so many people like me have gotten interested in old roses that many are available for sale over the internet. They include wild species, chinas, damasks, gallicas, eglantines, rugosas, wichuraianas, spinosissimas, musks, their hybrids, and more. They have to be rooted from twigs or root cuttings, so they aren't abundant and sell out quickly. Still, I've been able to snag my fair share.

That butterscotch rose underwent a change in this yard. In our alkaline native soil, its buds open to white, especially in warmer weather, and sometimes the buds are even tinged with pink. It's a phenomenon that's much more familiar with hydrangeas. Acid soil gives them blue flowers. In our yard, they bloom only pink or white.

The Railroad Rose.

A law school classmate told me that he could trace the historical developments of little towns along railroad routes through the west by looking at laws enacted along the way — including laws treating the spreading of noxious weeds. In a way, I have seen how one weed followed a railroad.

The weed is a rose species, probably *Rosa Canina*, the dog rose. It's a wild plant named for the sturdy hooked thorns that line its limbs, like a dog's teeth. Clumps of the rose stud the fields along the route of the old Cedar River Railroad east of Renton, Washington, southeast of Seattle. I've rooted it from a start and it grows 10 feet tall in my yard today. Its stiff, upright, and arching branches bloom with clusters of white, five-petalled flowers each spring, then develop thick clusters of bright red hips.

Old Garden Roses

Old Garden Roses (OGR) is the term given to species that have been cultivated in Europe and the mid-East for centuries. Most develop as dense shrubs with multiple canes emerging from the ground. They are tough enough to have withstood the cold winters and hot dry summers for centuries. Most are dense with petals, mostly pink to dark magenta, most with heavy, sweet perfume. Story has it that during the Napoleonic era (1879-1815), even while England and France waged war against one another, rose aficionados traded rose starts across their national borders. One is called Malmaison, named after the Chateau Malmaison, where Napoleon's Josephine kept her rose garden. Similarly, the French breeder of the hybrid tea "Peace rose" of 1945 sent it out of France to assure that it survived WWII's German invasion.

When I first became interested in types of roses, hybridizers had perfected the hybrid tea with its few woody canes, single solitary flowers, and brilliant flowers — but many newer varieties had lost the most iconic trait of all, their perfumes. I planted OGRs in my yard for their fragrance: they include two French varieties, Reine de Violettes and Belle de Crecy; a centifolia, "the Cabbage rose" named for its high petal count; Rose de Rescht, a youngster introduced in 1880; Zepherine Drouhin which has no thorns; and others I collected from alleys and abandoned farmyards whose names I'll never know.

Moss Roses

Among the OGRs in my yard are two moss roses, Common Moss and Henri Martin (probably; I'll never know for sure, because I collected it from a ditch. It's a rose bush, not to be confused with portulaca, the little ground-hugging flower called "moss rose.") Moss roses have a genetic distinction — their buds are covered with greenery that looks like moss. My common moss came from my maternal grandmother to my mother. I kept it weeded for her, but not easily, because the many stems it sends up from the ground are completely covered with prickles.

I found Henri Martin, a red moss, growing in a ditch along Highway 101 just south of my hometown of Florence, Oregon. My sister Tina helped me gather the start. The rose was just a weed, not close to any house or yard, not cared for. I pulled my car onto the shoulder of the highway and Tina jumped out to break off a twig. To tease her, I yelled, "Run!" as though somebody were chasing us. She leaped back in the car, but twisted her back so that she hurt for days. That rose rooted easily, because, "If you steal a start, it's sure to grow."

Austrian Copper

Another start I purloined is Austrian Copper. It has naturalized in the Wenatchee Valley and in other parts of North Central Washington. I collected my start from a root cutting growing in an embankment between a road and an abandoned farm. It puts out a spectacular show of color in the spring. Its flowers have only five petals each, but the plant covers itself with flowers. The outside of the petals are yellow. The inside is red-orange, just like that color in a box of Crayola Crayons. The bush is the color of flames when it's in bloom, then it sets a heavy crop of orange hips. It is big, thorny, and dense. It also mutates—sometimes a branch puts out flowers that are plain yellow, front and back.

When Shakespeare's Juliet said, "A rose by any other name would smell as sweet," she wasn't thinking of Austrian Copper. It is a variety of *Rosa foetida*, named "fetid" because it stinks.

Father Hugo's Rose

Some of my roses are historical, but not quite as old as the OGRs. One is Father Hugo's Rose, *Rosa Hugonis*, a species from China. It was collected by Hugh Scanlan, an Irish Franciscan priest. He sent its seeds to the Kew Botanical Gardens in London. Every year, it is the first rose to bloom in my garden, covering its thin arching canes with yellow flowers.

Harrison's Yellow

Harrison's Yellow resembles Austrian Copper, but it is plain yellow. It is said to be the Yellow Rose of Texas. It was bred by a rose-growing lawyer in New York City in the 1830s by crossing a yellow *Rosa foetida*, Persian Yellow, with a stickery Scotch briar rose, a *spinosissima*. In the 1840s, settlers in wagon trains carried it into the west. It's the big, mounding yellow rose that appears in the spring-time around old homesteads in Central Washington.

Climbing American Beauty

My Climbing American Beauty rose, dating from 1909, is technically a "trailing rose" or "rambling rose" because its long canes are lax rather than tall and stiff. It blooms with deep pink smallish flowers, small at least compared to hybrid teas. It has glossy leaves with rounded tips, and a strong sweet fragrance. I've started it for my son, who remembers it as the rose at the Seattle house where he grew up. It is thriving in his yard in Richmond, Virginia. I'm glad I've outsourced it so that I have a source to go to, should mine fail.

Dr. Van Fleet or New Dawn

Stuck in a spot in my yard where I have room to prop-agate starts, I am watching a small start of either Dr. Van Fleet, from 1899, or its sport (mutant), New Dawn, from 1930. Dr. Van Fleet has pale pink flowers, glossy leaves with rounded tips, and long trailing vines. It blooms once each spring. New Dawn looks the same, but blooms re-peatedly. It is popular enough that it is still available in plant nurseries.

The Rugosas

Rugosa roses, blooming deep pink, yellow, or white, grow to rounded shrubs with crinkled leaves that look like mint. They smell sweet. They are as tough as nails. Some, like the Hansa in my yard, are noted for setting fat red hips that are useful for making rose hip tea. Ironically, the Thomas Lipton in my yard, named for the founder of the Lipton Tea company, sets only small, black hips that are useless for beverages.

Fragrant Red Roses

The stereotype of a rose is red and fragrant, sweet-smelling like the OGRs but less musky and much fruitier, like peaches. A set of hybrid teas that fits that ideal is still available on the market, and I have had them in my yard, growing under the names of Mr. Lincoln, Chrysler Imperial, Oklahoma, and Mirandy.

My mother used to recite,

When God gave out noses

I thought He said "roses"

And I said

I'll take a big red one.

Modern Beauties

I don't ignore modern hybrid teas in my garden, although I don't seek them out and I don't rely on them to be hearty. Still, very fragrant Perfume Delight and Tiffany are earning their places in my garden. I've read that the newer type of hybrid shrubs from David Austen in Britain are hearty, dense, and fragrant, so if space ever develops in my garden, I might try one.

Why Collect?

Collecting roses is a hobby, or a passion, or an obsession, depending on who is judging whom. Some of my collection is purely sentimental, like the Moss Rose my grandmother grew, the Dorothy Perkins that grows along the river in my hometown of Florence, Oregon, and the Dr. Van Fleet my mother grew. When I started collecting, I was concerned that roses, like commercial apples of the same era, would lose their appeal forever. I'm happy that so many Old Garden Roses and have commercial growers today — now it won't have to be up to me to save them for posterity. My collection won't suffer the fate like that of a friend at Snoqualmie, Washington, who collected starts of antique apples. A herd of elk moved into his neighborhood and ate them.

CHAPTER 30

Tomatoes versus Fruit Flies

When we moved to Wenatchee, I was thrilled to be coming to a place that was warm enough for me to grow tomatoes, if only in a couple of 3 X 8 foot raised flower beds on our small lot. My knowledgeable neighbors must have chuckled when I grossly overplanted, but what did I know?

I installed a dozen plants in the raised beds, and six more in our flower beds. I had never seen a tomato plant that was taller than about 2-½ feet, so I was amazed when my plants grew riotously. Soon they were taller than I am. They overwhelmed the flimsy bamboo stakes I had used to prop their limbs, sprawled across the ground, and kept on growing.

By mid-August I had tomatoes ripening at a rate of about 10 pounds per day. We cooked them down into tomato sauce with Italian seasonings. We had visions of spaghetti marinara, lasagna, eggplant parmesan, chicken cacciatore, anything else Italian that Lidia Bastianich cooked on TV, plus pizza of course.

Then I decided to get fancy and dry tomatoes in a dehydrator. I calculated my savings over the price of gourmet sun-dried tomatoes at the supermarket. I set up the dehydrator outdoors on my BBQ table, checked it a few times, then forgot about it for the rest of the day.

Remembering the dehydrator after sundown, I carried it indoors and took off the lid. A cloud of fruit flies came streaming into the house. I rushed it back outdoors and slammed the door, but I was too slow — a cloud of flies flitted through the kitchen. By morning, they had migrated to the windows, where I attacked them with a vacuum cleaner. Then I took a garden hose to the dehydrator trays, which were loaded with a shocking volume of fly biomass. Another whole cloud of flies relocated to my compost pile to feast on the ersatz sun-dried tomatoes that I had to discard.

I'm back to cooking my tomatoes. I've learned my lesson about fruit flies. If they get indoors, a friend advised, catch them in a glass of wine or dish of vinegar. In an outdoor battle between me and them over my tomatoes, they win.

CHAPTER 31

A Saga of Rescue Tomatoes

I know people who have soft spots in their hearts for rescue animals. My son Eric adopted a dog rescued in New Orleans after Hurricane Katrina. My friend Cathy went straight to Animal Control when her poodle died and came home with another. My husband Jerry has befriended a roving tomcat who checks in with him daily, sometimes climbing on his lap for a quick catnap before returning to his rounds.

My propensity is different. I am a sucker for rescue plants. A neighbor gave me a sprig of chocolate mint that I rooted and grew into a mature plant. It's invasive. I retrieved an iris rhizome from the pile of yard waste that somebody dumped over a fence. I bought another corm at the Pybus Public Market, cheap because it was all bloomed out. I had to cultivate the two just to learn what colors they were. They have divided profusely.

And I have rescue tomatoes. I don't need them, didn't want them. I've had experiences with tomatoes.

I spent the first sixty-two years of my life on the wet side of the Cascades where a growing tomato was an exotic plant. I grew one plant in a pot cozied up to the garage door because that was the warmest place in my garden. It produced just one red, round, unblemished tomato. It was perfect for plucking on the very day that Jerry and I weren't home. His stepmother, a gourmet, recognized what a treasure it was, so she picked it and ate it.

When I was a kid, occasionally my mother would buy a large beefsteak tomato, slice it, serve it, and savor it as salad for the whole family at dinner. In August, a truck farmer from Yakima, Washington, would drive slowly down our street. All the kids playing in the sand lots nearby would run home to tell their mothers. Moms would hurry outside with their billfolds to buy fresh produce. For us, that meant a 50 pound gunnysack of green beans for canning, a 23 pound box of apples for applesauce, a flat of tomatoes for stewed tomatoes, and a quart carton of cherry tomatoes to eat fresh. They were pungent and acrid and could be weaponized: If you bit a cherry tomato just right, you could squirt seeds at your brother.

When I moved to Wenatchee I discovered heritage tomatoes, those flavorful homestead varieties not grown commercially because they don't keep well or look perfect. The man at the feedstore said that "Mrs. Maxwell's Big Red Italian" was a favorite. He was sold out, but I found a grower in Idaho who would send me ten seeds if I sent him a self-addressed envelope. While those seeds germinated, I brought home a couple more varieties, "Stupice" and "Siletz," both supposed to be good for our climate. Then a friend gave me seeds for "San Marzano," supposed to be best for Italian sauces. All told, I had about eighteen plants. My niece, who grew up raising tomatoes in Arizona, chuckled knowingly.

I had no idea that tomato plants could be so productive. That summer I had more tomatoes than I could eat, can, freeze or dry. Eventually—thank goodness—I found that Hospitality House (now Wenatchee Rescue Mission) would accept donations of fresh produce. Wasting food was not an option. That's a sin.

I swore I would never grow so many tomato plants again. I gave my dehydrator to a man with a medical marijuana license and I donated my quart canning jars to the Wenatchee Senior Activity Center Thrift Shop. I contented myself planting just a handful of "Mrs. Maxwell" seeds, hoping for two strong plants for the raised flower beds in my front yard.

But then I saw six little tomato plants, sitting in their little nursery cups, all lined up along our street for anybody to take home. I watched them shiver in the wind all afternoon. Everybody ignored them. Night was falling and the temperature would soon drop below freezing. I scooped up all six and carried them home to my heated garage. I repotted them into bigger pots with nutritious potting soil and set them under grow lights with my "Mrs. Maxwell" seedlings. They thrived.

I asked the neighbor why he had abandoned them. "Wrong variety," he said. They are "Better Boy," an indeterminate variety that will grow taller than I am, then keep on growing until frost nips them.

So there I was with no more quart canning jars and six big healthy plants. I may have a soft spot in my heart for rescue plants; or is the soft spot in my head?

CHAPTER 32

Weeds

Birds and wind bring seeds into the yard, some of which lay down roots where they land. Typically, they are weeds — plants that tolerate harsh environments and produce prodigious amounts of seed. When I have found a volunteer that I don't recognize, I have treated it like an honored guest, at least until it blooms, then I dig out my botany books.

My modern books are aimed at our region, are filled with full color photographs, and are organized by the color of flowers. If I can't find a matching flower there, I resort to the technique I learned as a college freshman in 1965. I bring out a hand lens, a dictionary, a razor blade, and a dichotomous key. First, I need to remember what the shape of a complex flower is called — is this one an umbel, a panicle, a corymb, or a raceme? Then I have to count the sepals, petals, stigmas, stamens, and pistils. I slice the flower vertically. Is the ovary superior or inferior to the ring of sepals and petals? I slice horizontally. How many cells are there in the ovary? Then I have to apply judgment. Would I say these petals are fused or fully independent of one another? Would I say this color is white, or is it tinted? And so on.

Now I apply the key, which is like following an IRS tax form. The key offers at least two choices on each line. For example, is the plant herbaceous or woody? Herbaceous, so skip entries for woody plants, and go to herbaceous plants at line X below. At line X, decide: Do the leaves make a basal rosette or not? No? Okay skip to line XX below. At line XX, keep making judgement. Are the petals adhered, or not? And keep going and going until I reach the end of the choices. Does my flower look like the rather rough drawing in the book? If I've made even one misinterpretation along the way, I haven't identified the plant.

What's amazing is that thousands of plants, even in a single region, have been identified to that degree. What's also amazing is that many smaller plants have not been identified to any degree. And along comes DNA and re-attributes plants to families that nobody thought they belonged to before.

The volunteer plants in my garden have brought both some bad juju and some fun. I bought a package of seeds that were supposed to be Artemesia *absintha* (the wormwood that is used for absinthe), which can be found wild around here. The seeds produced something with artemisia-type leaves, like native sagebrush, but they were not *absintha* and had no aroma at all. They did produce lavish amounts of seed that germinated in every expansion joint in my driveway all the way down to the street.

Wild sunflowers volunteer. They pop up everywhere, in flowerbeds and out of them, in the compost, in some other plant's pots. They are very welcome. When I planted huge hybrid sunflowers, they grew to 8 feet tall, then in one day, all died. It appears they were killed by a fungal infection. My research indicated that I should never plant sunflowers in the same place again. Luckily, the wild sunflowers are just as sunny, and seem immune to the fungal infection.

Evening scented primrose pops up and gets to survive because it's pretty.

One of my strangers turned out to be Spikeweed (*Hemizonia pungens*), a short green plant so covered with spiney bracts that it looked like a cactus with yellow flowers. It wasn't showy enough to keep and grow like a flower.

Another was Giant Ragweed (*Ambrosia trifida*). Luckily, I identified it before it bloomed and gave everybody hay fever.

REFERENCES

Gilkey, Helen: *Handbook of Northwest Flowering Plants, Second Edition,* Binfords & Mort, Portland, OR (1961). This 414-page dichotomous key with line drawings cost me $4.00 new.

Niehaus, Theodore F. and Ripper, Charles L.: *Pacific States Wildflowers, Peterson Field Guides,* Houghton Mifflin Co., Boston and New York (1976).

Turner, Mark and Gustafson, Phyllis: *Wildflowers of the Pacific Northwest,* Timber Press, Inc. Portland, OR (2006).

Camp, Pamela and Gamon, John: *A Field Guide to the Rare Plants of Washington,* University of Washington Press, Seattle and London (2011).

CHAPTER 33

Dandelions

The dandelion gets a bad rap for being a pest. It sends out its rosette of basal leaves in the middle of an otherwise smooth monoculture of lawn. It thrusts its taproot deep into the soil of the flower bed or in the middle of a rock path, too deep to yank out. A yank breaks it off and it comes back from the root. It produces prodigious amounts of seed that is well-adapted to sail in the wind. And it is tougher than nails, loving lush habitats, but tolerating hostile hot, cold, and dry circumstances. In short, it is a weed.

But the dandelion is also a beauty that everybody recognizes from early childhood on. And who hasn't plucked a stem and blown on the puffy balls of seeds that the flowers become? It happens to be completely edible, although I've never known a human to eat one. Chickens and Guinea pigs are ravenous for their greens.

Some years ago, I read that in Great Britain, gardeners had rooted out dandelions so zealously that the plant had become rare and endangered. Evidently that was not true—I see mention on the internet today that dandelions and dozens of flowers in their same genus are thriving in Great Britain.

One dandelion in my yard is safe from overzealous gardening. It germinated in the crack between two concrete blocks in my retaining wall, in the second tier down. The root expanded in the space like a molly bolt expanded behind a wall. The blocks are too heavy for me to lift, so the dandelion thrives there undisturbed. From early spring on, it blooms for me regularly.

Sci-Fi writer Ray Bradbury named one of his classics *Dandelion Wine*. That inspired me to collect a bucket full of the flowers from the floor of an orchard, thinking that I'd try to make wine. However, the damp mass molded before I found a recipe or instructions, and I realized, also, that the orchard had been sprayed. I had no idea what was in the spray—something for apple maggots, at the least—and no idea how persistent any spray might be from tree to ground to seed to stem to flower. I'll have to get my wine from a commercial source. Better the known devil.

CHAPTER 34

Grasses

When I was a lawyer, I played second chair counsel in a federal court case. In short, our client had been sued by the U.S. Corps of Engineers for disturbing a wetland on the edge of the Swinomish Channel in Skagit County, Washinton. The land in question was a triangular 11-acre former strawberry field bordered by a highway, the channel, and a railroad. It sat below sea level behind a hundred-year-old dike and was underlain by drainage pipes and flapper valves that dumped water into the channel at low tide.

The COE deemed the parcel to be a wetland:

Wetlands are areas that are inundated or saturated by surface or ground water at a frequency and duration sufficient to support, and that under normal circumstances do support, a prevalence of vegetation typically adapted for life in saturated soil conditions. Wetlands generally include swamps, marshes, bogs, and similar areas.

The plant that grew in the field that the COE identified as wetland plant was a grass, *Agrostis alba*. We won the case by showing that *Agrostis alba* was not particularly adapted to tolerate saturated soil conditions like certain reeds and rushes were. Rather, it would grow anywhere. It was used by the State of Washington to reseed construction projects because it was tough and tolerant of many environments. Our expert witness pulled a bunch of *Agrostis alba* out of his jacket pocket during trial and swore under oath that he had pulled it from the lawn of the federal courthouse, right outside the doors of our courtroom.

After coming to the Wenatchee Valley, I worked on a project with the Nature Conservancy. A team of five of us drove out onto the shrub-steppe to spend a day harvesting the seeds of native bunch grass. The seed would be delivered to a farmer, who would grow a seed crop for the Nature Conservancy to use in habitat restoration projects.

Bunch grass is a native perennial plant that grows in clumps and sends down deep roots to reach scant desert moisture. Its enemy is cheat grass—Bunch grass gets crowded out by annual spreading grasses that hog the spring moisture, then dry out by summer, contributing fuel to wildfires.

Our group leader started out by showing us how to identify the plants whose seeds we would be collecting. A botany graduate student in our group said that his class on grasses was one of his most difficult—maybe not because of the botany involved, but because he was allergic to grass.

Grasses, like any flowering plant, can be identified by examination of their flowers, but also, by the subtle ways in which their leaves wrap around their stems. We weren't as subtle as all that. We looked for clumps of grasses with seed heads adorned by long fibers that extend from the top of seeds, called "awns." (Think of depictions of heads of wheat; typically, they show off long awns.)

Five of us picked all day but filled a 5-gallon bucket no more than half full.

When the wind passes over bunch grasses and combs the awns, the grass sways in a beautiful dance. When I mentioned the beauty of the awns to two of my friends, they were horrified. Some awns are auger-shaped so that the wind whips them into the ground like little drills. A veterinarian told of having to treat dogs with awns drilled into their eyes, mouths, and throats. And an acquaintance said that whenever his dog got into prairie grass, that meant an immediate trip to the vet.

I allow the prairie grasses to develop on the steep cutbank on the face of my lot. It's too steep for anybody to walk dogs there.

REFERENCE:

Whitson, Tom D., Ed.: *Weeds of the West, 5th Edition*, Newark, CA, The Western Society of Weed Scientists and University of Wyoming (1996).

CHAPTER 35

Tumbleweeds

It's spring, so the tumbleweeds break free
from winter-rotted roots
and take a ride on the breeze.
They bounce as lightly as toy balloons,
rolling wherever the wind will blow,
even up hill
until they hit a fence, and stay a while.

Where the bureaucrats see noxious weeds,
I see them bounce, and they make me smile.

Spring announces itself in the high desert with days of
dazzling sunlight interspersed with the last flurries of winter snow. Creeks that plunge out of the narrow canyons
between the foothills are full to their brims with meltwa-
ter from the snowpack. Birds reappear, including Robins,

flocks of Red-winged Blackbirds and Starlings. The Northern Flickers find resonant tree-trunks, poles, and metal roofs to drum resolutely in search of mates. Even before the thin skin of spring greenery appears on brown hills, we see tumbleweeds.

Tumbleweeds are the dead and desiccated brown twigs of last year's bushes the size and shape and weight of beach balls, stickery to handle. Dusted with snow, they are a beautiful sphere of lace.

In the wind, the tumbleweed bounces along the path of least resistance, across fields, along roads, down railroads, even uphill if that's where the wind is going.

A tumbleweed is indeed a "weed," an unwanted plant that tolerates even hostile environmental conditions and produces prodigious quantities of seeds. The tumbleweed's method of dispersing seed, by rolling, is relatively unusual among the plants of the world, compared to the number of plants that spread their seeds by dribbling them onto the ground, like fennel, or casting them to the wind on plumes like dandelions, or encasing them in fruit for birds to gobble and disperse like Saskatoon berries, or floating them away like coconuts.

Although their method of distributing seeds is relatively unusual, still they can come from a number of families, including so-called Tumbling Pigweed (*Amaranthaceae,* amaranth), Tumbling Mustard (*Brassicaceae,* mustard), florist's Baby's Breath (*Caryophyllacea),* Mediterranean Sage (*Lamiceae,* mint or *Salvia*), and White Knapweed (*Asteraceae,* aster). However, the epitome of the tumbleweed is the Prickly Russian Thistle (sometimes called an *Amaranthaeceae* or sometimes *Chenopodiaceae,* goosefoot family.)

Each tumbleweed grows from a single stem that weakens over winter and breaks off at ground level in March winds. The plants roll away, shedding thousands of seeds along their paths. Somebody with the patience to count them has reported that a single tumbleweed can produce 250,000 seeds.

Tumbleweeds can be nuisances, but technically, they are not "noxious." A noxious weed is one that has been declared by the government to be a plant that is injurious to agricultural and horticultural crops, natural habitats, ecosystems, humans, or livestock. Either a local government or the federal government can declare a plant to be noxious, but neither the US DA nor the governments of the western states have declared it to be "noxious." California has listed two other Russian thistles, but not "Prickly." Perhaps prickly Russian thistle hasn't been declared to be a noxious weed because it has naturalized so vastly — it is so widespread that any effort to control it would be futile.

Tumbleweed are nuisances because they can compete with agricultural crops for water in the arid west. Unlike a compact barrel cactus, their twiggy form exposes so much area to evaporation that they can suck up 44 gallons of water during a single growing season. They can also pile up so high that they stack against buildings and fill yards high enough to be fire hazards, and they can block highways. In December 2019, tumbleweeds covered a highway in south central Washington State so deeply that the road was shut down for 10 hours while the State Department of Transportation deployed snowplows to move them.

Tumbleweeds have not always been pests. The Prickly Russian Thistle came from the Ukraine. There, where it was cultivated in alkaline soils, it absorbed sodium carbonate and potassium carbonate that were refined from its ashes after it was burned. The sodium carbonate, in turn, was used to control the temperature in kilns melting silica to make glass. Its use in glassmaking was known in Egyptian and Roman times. Mixed with lye, the ash made soap. Its use in soap was documented in a Babylonian clay tablet dating from 2200 BC.

Like the Ukraine, Spain also refined burned Prickly Russian Thistle, and its glass-making industry was so important to the nation that exporting Prickly Russian Thistle seeds to a possible competitor was illegal. However, in 1793, a chemical method of creating sodium carbonate was developed, and the plant lost its industrial value.

Prickly Russian Thistle arrived in the United States in the 1870s as a contaminant in a shipment of flaxseed to Bonhomme County, South Dakota. It quickly spread throughout the U.S. It wasn't totally useless — historian Tim Egan writes in *The Worst Hard Time* that people ate its tender young shoots when gardens dried up during the Dust Bowl era. It can be grown as a hay crop on arid soils, especially since it takes so little water to germinate, and even after germination, if it dries, its seedlings can rehydrate and survive. It has enough nutritional value that agriculturists who would monetize it say that it is underutilized.

In the 1930s, the tumbleweed entered the American cultural conscious as a symbol of the old west. That happened when Bob Nolan wrote a song called "Tumbling Along Like a Tumbling Tumbleweed." In 1934, his song was a hit for the Sons of the Pioneers with vocalist Roy Rogers. Since then, an impressive array of other musicians have covered the song, including   crooner Bing Crosby, yodeler Slim Whitman, Pat Boone, Johnny Ray, Lorne Greene from the TV show "Bonanza," Kate Smith famous for "God Bless America," The Supremes with Diana Ross as lead vocalist, Clint Eastwood, Frankie Laine famous for "Mule Train," and Michael Nesmith of The Monkees. You can also hear the song in the movie "The Big Lewbowski." So, it seems that nothing is likely to disturb the invasive tumbleweed's beloved status.

REFERENCES

Bernau, C.R. and E.P. Eldredge: *Plant Guide, for Prickly Russian Thistle (Solana tragus I.)*, 2018, USDA-Natural Resource Conservation Service, Great Basin Plant Materials Center. Fallon, NV.

Egan, Timothy: *The Worst Hard Time,* Houghton Mifflin Co. Boston (2006)

Whitson, Thomas, Editor, et al.: *Weeds of the West,* 5th Edition, Newark, CA, The Western Society of Weed Science. (1996)

https://plants.usda.gov/java/noxious (accessed March 25, 2020)

CHAPTER 36

¡Ah, Composte!

It takes an avid gardener to get excited about compost. Gardeners discuss, argue, and boast about their compost piles. They aren't satisfied to compost in pretty gallon-sized containers advertised in *Gorgeous House* type magazines. What would that generate, about two tablespoons of dirt? Rather, they build side-by-side corrals from kits holding a cubic yard of waste each. They have no trouble filling them with garden trimmings from a single urban lot.

At least that's my experience.

I follow instructions from composting experts: I combine green grass trimmings and brown leaves, turn the mixture over frequently to keep it aerated, keep out the seeds of invasive weeds, and keep it damp.

The first challenge of composting here in North Central Washington is keeping the compost damp. Our precipitation averages seven inches per year. A cartoonist would envision us as being acres of sand and saguaro cacti with their arms lifted waving "Hi," among bleached out cow skulls. We have acres of sagebrush, a few low-growing cacti, and massive irrigation systems. If I didn't irrigate it, my compost would desiccate and fascinate some future archeologist or anthropologist: "Look here! Remains of hollyhocks, gladiolas. Once this desert was wet. This proves there was climate change!" I irrigate my compost pile as regularly as I water the peonies and roses.

The second challenge is keeping out the seedy weeds. Around here, that includes tumbleweeds.

Every spring, the wind dislodges all the tumbleweeds from an undeveloped lot next to mine and dumps them in my backyard. They fill an entire corner of the yard three feet deep. Experts say that a single tumbleweed will produce a quarter of a million seeds. I jump on the plants to crunch them up small enough to fit in bags for garden trash, but as I crush them, they drop half their seeds before I can get their stickery twigs bagged up. I may have a better idea: I'll wait for a windy day, then roll them out of my backyard, past the length of the house, all the way to the front yard, then out onto the street. Then I'll let the wind carry them away. They could roll for blocks until they met their next obstacle. I'll tell people it's a race—I'm taking bets on which goes farthest. Do you want to give your favorite tumbleweed a name, like Weedy McTumble?

My compost pile smells sweet with yard trimmings: Oregano, thyme, five kinds of mint (spearmint, peppermint, horehound, catnip mint, chocolate mint), bronze fennel that smells like licorice, and a pinch of cedar from hedge trimming. In the case of an occasional rotten potato or onion from the kitchen, I toss a handful of dirt on it. Earthworms just love finding something gooey like that in compost.

As for those earthworms: Experts say they aren't indigenous. They arrived with the Europeans in New England, and ever since, they've invaded forests, forded the Mississippi, crossed the plains, climbed over the Rockies, and found my backyard compost pile. They've traversed the continent in the blink of an eye, in geological terms. They've survived extreme conditions, even though experts say they can't tolerate the sun's ultraviolet rays. Earthworms are good for churning garden soil, so if I dig one up, I return it at once to keep it from getting sunburned.

I haven't uncovered any nightcrawlers, those bigger earthworms with flattened tails. I've hoped to dig up a Giant Palouse earthworm, and I might have. I dug up one worm that was so big that if I were a girly-girl, I would have screamed when I saw it. It was at least 15 cm long (that's only about six inches when it's scrunched up, but it sounds more dramatic in centimeters). It was as fat as a caterpillar or grub. It was pinkish on one end, fading almost to blue on the other. I should have taken a picture to show an expert.

An American Robin claims the compost pile as its own. I hope it doesn't try to swallow that big worm; it might choke.

The compost pile surprises me by growing plants from seeds that birds or breezes bring in. A squash vine bloomed in the compost, clambered over the fence and up into the neighbor's tree overhanging my yard, and produced fruits that hung like Chinese lanterns decorating the yard for a garden party.

My compost pile sits in the southeast corner of my yard, where it borders part of the northwest corner of my neighbor's lot. Our yards are separated by a four-foot-high solid board fence. I haven't met those neighbors yet. They are usually away at work, and I speak only English while they speak only Spanish. When we meet, I'm sure we'll get along: they compost their lawn trimmings. One Saturday when I spent hours bending and digging and sifting compost into a bucket to spread, they could see only my head bobbing up and down beyond the fence. When I took a quick break, the woman peeked over the fence to see what I was doing. Approvingly, "¡Ah, composte!" I heard her say.

REFERENCE:

Sampson, Susan Rae: "Too Rare To Be Endangered, the Ironic Status of the Giant Palouse Earthworm Under the Endangered Species Act," *Awake in the World,* Livingston, MT, Riverfeet Press (2017)

CHAPTER 37

On Meditation and Earworms in my Garden

Meditation is supposed to be good for us, and gardening is supposed to be a meditative experience, but I'm not sure that I understand meditation. Genetically, I'm physically restless; I can't do the mind-focusing type of meditation that requires me to sit cross-legged on a mat and chant "Om mani padme hum." I'm moderately more successful at meditation that involves being observant and respectful of living things, especially in the natural (unbuilt) world. My mind is most open to ideas when I am working in my garden; I wonder if that is meditation.

Garden tasks in my small yard are repetitious, but rarely strenuous. Since I am usually weeding, my acts are not consistent with respect for all life that is part of some meditative teachings. To me, plants, fungi, lichens, slime molds and kelp are just as imbued with a sense of a life force as are the insects, field mice, birds, and the rare slug that I encounter in the garden. But some of the plants encroach upon my gardening lifestyle, and I have to pull them out.

Others who meditate have come to grips with killing weeds. I've seen many photographs of monasteries supporting meditative lifestyles, but I've never seen one that was overrun with weeds. (Be honest: Haven't you wondered how the monks keep cats from digging up their zen gardens of perfectly raked sand?)

Recently, instead of killing weeds, I've been depositing them in the part of my yard that is natural and hoping they grow there. That part of the yard, the embankment along the street, is left natural because it's too steep for me to work on. I hate it when my neighbors empty their lawn mowers over their banks just to dispose of grass so I do it neatly so it doesn't show. Saving the weeds fits nicely into the trend that environmentalists are encouraging me to try — letting part of the yard be natural to support native insects for the sake of supporting native birds.

When I am engaging in the tedium of pulling weeds, my mind goes into freefall. I let it go. It might take me anywhere. It has no particular theme. I "go with the flow" and that is rewarding enough to steer me back into the garden day after day, year after year. It's been that way since I was a child, when pulling weeds was one of my assigned chores. That was like throwing Brer Rabbit in the briar patch; he was happiest there. My sister was envious because she didn't enjoy any of our chores, but I suspect she meditated — I called it "daydreaming," and sometimes she was so lost in her daydream that I accused her of falling into a trance.

But mentally going with the flow doesn't always flow perfectly. I encounter "earworms," those involuntary and intrusive phrases from song or speech recalled over and over again with maddening frequency. I heard of "earworms" first in a newspaper column by the humorist Dave Barry. It was part of his 1997 quest to list the worst songs ever, in *Dave Barry's Book of Bad Songs*. The book opens with a warning about earworms. It says the book "will put bad songs into your head," and suggests that instead of perusing it, the reader should give it to enemies to plant the bad songs in their heads instead, as acts of psychological warfare.

To me, earworms take the form of rhythmic speech, like the name "Letitia Macapinlac" which is the name of a woman I met only once over 40 years ago, or "John Hockenberry" who is a radio journalist. I can also be troubled by a folk song like "Where are you going, Billy boy, Billy boy, where are you going charming Billy?" or a snippet from pop rock, "Smoke on the water, fire in the sky...."

What if scientists determined that earworms were actual living organisms, like athlete's foot? I could get a visit from the Environmental Protection Agency: "Put down the pitchfork, M'am. We're just here to protect your earworm. Other people's earworms sing 'Smoke on the Water,' but yours sings 'Letitia Macapinlac.' It might be rare and endangered."

I need to crowd Letitia out of my mind before the EPA can finish my brain scan. I need to think of something louder, rowdier to crowd her out. I can't remember the words to "Om mani padme hum." I don't know the other words from "Smoke on the Water." I think so hard I can hear my brain gears turning. Goodbye, Letitia! Now I am obsessing over "What shall we do with the drunken sailor, what shall we do with the drunken sailor, what shall we do with the drunken sailor, early in the morning."

CHAPTER 38

Pesticides and GMOs

I was at college, sitting in a student lounge, about to bite into a shiny, big, red apple, when a fellow student said, "You know, don't you, that the shiny ones are poison?" I froze and we both laughed. I immediately thought of a Disney witch with a green complexion and a crooked nose tendering a shiny red apple to a gullible Snow White.

Food crops, like shiny red apples, get sprayed with pesticides for bacterial, fungal, and insect infestations. The sprays can't always be washed off. They wouldn't be effective if wind and rain could knock them off. I don't know what happens to them after they are absorbed into leaves, stems, or bark. My brother the ER physician was working in Bakersfield, California, when people were sickened from eating watermelon they'd purchased from a roadside stand. The toxin had not penetrated the hard, washed, rind of the watermelon, but it had penetrated the meat of the melon through the soft stem scar.

I have seen a beautiful crop of watercress blooming the water in a drainage swale (ditch) next to a hiking trail. I observed that the water was downhill from a roadway exposed to automobile pollutant. In all probability, the shoulders of the road had been sprayed with herbicides, as well.

My college botany professor and his dog got sick from eating puffball mushrooms that he had picked from his lawn. I wonder if he thought about what chemicals he'd used to cultivate that lawn?

I do not know what is contained in the sprays that keep our food crops free from pests. However, I am sympathetic to the farmer or orchardist who needs to protect a crop from fire blight or apple maggots, for example. In my county, orchardists are legally required to maintain their trees, whether organically or otherwise, and must remove an orchard rather than abandon it, because of the risk of infestations that one grower can cause another. And we all have to eat.

On the other hand, I do have concerns about misuse and over-use. We, society in general, have a history of misusing DDT. It's an old story—we sprayed DDT and saved a large human population from the mosquito-born malaria protozoan, but simultaneously, we seriously decimated the Bald Eagle population. DDT made the shells of its eggs, and eggs of other birds, too fragile to remain intact until a chick could hatch. Fortunately, Rachel Carson alerted us to the problem in her book *Silent Spring*, the use of DDT was reduced, and the Bald Eagle has recovered This isn't ancient history. All of it has occurred within my lifetime and within my memory.

Now, we have GMOs, genetically modified organisms. Frankly, in general, the concept of GMOs does not concern me at all. For millennia, humans have selected their finest plants and animals to propagate. Humans have cross-bred species or varieties to enhance products; that's hybridization. Creating a GMO simply effects that process at the genetic level without relying on random mutations to find a better trait in a plant. You needn't grow eighteen generations of Douglas-fir trees to breed one that tolerates heat better if you can do it by modifying genes in a single generation in the lab.

Errors have occurred in old-fashioned cross-breeding. For example, German Shepherd dogs have developed hip dysplasia as an adverse side-effect of their breeding. Similarly, unexpected results could result from creating GMOs, too, but with our ever-growing understanding of genetics, we know to watch for adverse side-effects before eighteen generations have passed.

The concern, of course, is misuse. For example, we hear about grain or corn being modified to withstand inundation with pesticides that will kill every other organism in their fields. That treats other organisms as collateral damage, and it is not okay. It's like killing human civilians to destroy a military installation.

In the interest of national security, humans have accepted civilian casualties as necessary evils of war. Witness Hiroshima or Dresden during WW II. In the realm of agriculture, we need to proceed conservatively. Nobody foresaw the side effects of DDT or Agent Orange. In the realm of agriculture, we don't need to wage war.

I am not growing food to feed the world in my yard, so I do not use pesticides. Luckily, the heat and wind keep most pests off my yard. I can brush away aphids with my fingers. Some friends have told me that if I need to manage powdery mildew on my rose bushes, I can spray them with milk. I can also change the environment to be incompatible with weeds by changing the pH of their soil without chemicals whose names I don't recognize.

My cousin Patty advises killing weeds that come up in joints in the driveway by dousing them with baking soda. When I objected to using Roundup in my yard, my husband bought a gallon of concentrated vinegar and a spray bottle for applying it judiciously. Sure, I can smell the aroma of pickles in my yard for a few days after I apply it to weeds in my rock pathways, but I prefer this over the alternative. Until I learn more, I feel like I am preserving what I want to keep in my garden without unnecessarily harming anything else.

CHAPTER 38

Wild Space

The long-curved side of my fan-shaped lot, except for the driveway, has gone natural. When I bought the lot in 2007, the flat top of the lot was a lawn extending from landscaping rocks at the base of the foundation of the house to the edge of a steep slope 10 feet down to the street. The slope had been shaved bare of foliage. Only Canadian thistle and tumbleweeds were sprouting up there. I'd prefer it to be vegetated because it's sandy and tends to erode.

Left alone, I'd expect the slope to be vegetated like the undeveloped strip of land across the street from me, growing between the street and a golf course. It grows sage brush, rabbit brush, and grasses. My slope has been more productive than that. It has sagebrush, rabbit brush, and prairie grasses, to be sure — but also has red-osier dogwood shrubs, Saskatoon (Service Berry) shrubs, and weeds like salsify, alfalfa, sweet clover, and buckwheat. It has filled in nicely, but not perfectly.

The revegetation still has a few bald spots, and has sprouted one invader, Siberian Elm. The elm is a fast-growing non-native tree that sends up invasive shoots. It caught my attention when it grew so high that it began to block our territorial view. At first, I just pruned it, but it was getting more and more difficult for me to stand on the steep slope using a power tool to cut it back. Eventually, I cut it to the ground. Even then, it tried to come back, sending a ring of green shoots from the cambium layer of the sawed-off stump.

The neighbors probably think I'm just being lazy for letting the cutbank go wild, but I'm much holier than that. By letting the slope go natural, I'm following the teachings of Douglas W. Tallamy, Ph.D., a professor of entomology and wildlife ecology. He advocates allowing at least part of our homesteads to grow naturally. He contends that plants, insects, and birds have co-evolved to thrive optimally when they grow together, helping preserve a diverse natural ecosystem.

The small natural part of my small yard might be too tiny to compensate for the loss of natural habitat beyond the cultivated part of my own yard, but Tallamy argues that if enough of us go natural, we will be significant contributors to conservation.

And I observe already that letting the bank go wild has lured birds in closer. A Black-capped chickadee calls from inside the dogwood and House Sparrows flit over its top. California Quail run among its trunks. An American Robin gorges on the Saskatoon berries.

How convenient that Tallamy's theory provides me a justification for letting my cutbank go wild; it isn't merely my laziness.

REFERENCE

Tallamy, Douglas W., *Nature's Best Hope: A New Approach to Conservation That Starts in Your Yard*, Portland, Timber Press (2019)

AFTERWORD

I entered my project of observing my yard expecting to see mostly what was already familiar to me. In terms of the variety of life I observed, largely that held true. However, looking closer and looking into my subjects widened my appreciation for the interconnectedness of nature, of local life with life around the region and around the world. It has increased my awe for the amazing development, persistence, and regeneration of life, its vulnerability and its endangerment. Observing has become a habit, and I do not foresee that abating.

ACKNOWLEDGMENTS

Some of these essays have appeared previously with slight editorial differences. My thanks to the *Wenatchee World* for "Tomatoes vs. Fruit Flies;" to *The Good Life* under Mike Cassidy, then the *Omak Chronical* for "Specialists," "Spiders," "Rescue Tomatoes," " ¡Ah, Composte!", "My Life With Insects;" and "On Meditation and Earworms in my Garden;" and to Wild Leek Press for my *Book of Birds.*

My thanks to poet Derek Sheffield for allowing me to quote from "The Seconds" from *Not For Luck,* Wheelbarrow Books, Michigan State University Press. Lansing, Michigan (2021).

My thanks to the good-natured members of the Castle Rock Writers Group who let me commandeer their time and attention for this project: Susan F. Blair, Mark Oswood, Merry Roy, and Ron Smith. The errors of grammar, spelling, syntax, science, and opinion are solely my own.

And my thanks to my husband Jerry Horn for his indulgence, whose preferred garden style would be to mow it all as bald and clean as a military haircut.

Susan Rae Sampson is a classical baby-boomer born in 1947, now a wife, a mother, and grandmother. She was raised in Florence, Oregon, on the coast, and got her college degrees from the University of Washington in Seattle (J.D. 1974, BA with Honors in English 1969.) She worked as a courtroom lawyer in the Seattle area for 35 years. She and her husband, a retired Skunkworks engineer, retired to North Central Washington in 2009. She is an active volunteer in the local chapter of the Audubon Society. She is an avid gardener, and in 2024 she completed coursework to become a certified master gardener through the Washington State University Extension Service.

As for writing, her Book of Birds won the first chapbook award from Wild Leek Press. With her son Brook Martin, she is the author of My Mom Had a Quilt Like That, a documentation of her collection of antique American patchwork quilts. She serves as Associate Editor of the Shrub-Steppe Poetry Journal, and works with Write on the River, an organization supporting writers in development. Her works have appeared in a handful of regional publications.